WORK HEALS EVERYTHING

WORK HEALS EVERYTHING

Life Lessons from a
First-Generation Entrepreneur

RAVINDRA NATH GOEL

RUPA

Published by
Rupa Publications India Pvt. Ltd 2026
161-B/4, Gulmohar House,
Yusuf Sarai Community Centre,
New Delhi 110049

Sales centres
Bengaluru Chennai
Hyderabad Kolkata Mumbai

P-ISBN: 978-93-7003-877-6
E-ISBN: 978-93-7003-123-4

First impression 2026

10 9 8 7 6 5 4 3 2 1

Printed in India

I dedicate this book to the memory of my parents, who brought me into this world, and to my very close friend, Dilip M. Salwi

CONTENTS

Foreword

The life of Dr Ravindra Nath Goel exemplifies the transformative power of entrepreneurship and technological innovation and showcases how one individual's passion and determination can revolutionize an industry's landscape. Dr Goel's transition from a scientist to an entrepreneur reflects his unwavering commitment to pushing the boundaries of possibility and creating positive change. His ability to blend scientific knowledge with practical application has not only reshaped the chemical industry but also inspired countless individuals to pursue their own entrepreneurial dreams.

As we delve into the pages of his memoir, we are not only treated to a fascinating tale of personal and professional triumph but also presented with a wealth of insights and lessons that can benefit aspiring entrepreneurs and technologists alike. His story serves as a beacon of hope and inspiration, reminding us of the boundless potential that lies within each of us to effect meaningful change and leave a lasting impact on the world.

I was captivated by the remarkable journey of this scientist who dared to venture beyond the confines and fetters of traditional academia by embarking upon a path that ultimately redefined the landscape of the chemical industry in India—especially the print and packaging industry. As a PhD holder from the prestigious Indian Institute of Technology (IIT) Delhi, Dr Goel possesses an innate curiosity and thirst for knowledge that propelled him towards ground-breaking discoveries as well as innovative products and solutions. Among these, his pioneering work in eco-friendly chemistry for the packaging industry not only demonstrates his technical expertise but also underscores his dedication to

environmental sustainability and social responsibility.

Even though my association with him began almost two decades ago, we became close when I assumed the role of vice chancellor at Deenbandhu Chhotu Ram University of Science & Technology (DCRUST), Murthal, Sonipat—one of the places where his factory is located.

I distinctly remember a phone call from Dr Goel many years ago, during which he introduced me to the company he had founded and elaborated on its product offerings. Initially, I had presumed it would be just another run-of-the-mill chemical company. However, upon visiting and engaging in discussions with him and his team, I was immediately struck by his extraordinary vision and capabilities. During our conversation, I enthusiastically suggested potential products for the printing and packaging industry, only to be met with Dr Goel's calm assertion that those products were already being developed and that some were even available in the market. His unwavering confidence and poise in asserting this fact left a profound impression on me. I couldn't help but marvel at his ingenuity, realizing that he had successfully created products that rivalled those of industry giants such as Henkel and H.B. Fuller. It was evident from that moment itself that Dr Goel was a force to be reckoned with—an individual whose innovative spirit and determination knew no bounds. I invited him to the board of governors of DCRUST and he accepted the same without any hesitation, as it was a service to the student community.

As our acquaintance grew, I discovered another facet of Dr Goel, that of him being a great poet. He has written classic poems in Hindi with great Indian philosophies. Once, at his place, I even found some interesting paintings adorning his walls and asked him where he had purchased them. He just smiled and took me to the next room, where I saw many paintings that were made by him and realized that he was a passionate painter. What a versatile genius! I was convinced that day that Dr Goel's journey is much more than just a chronicle of professional accomplishments.

I gradually came to recognize Dr Goel's esteemed reputation as an innovative scientist. Numerous stalwarts within the printing industry spoke highly of his remarkable achievements and contributions. I discovered Dr Goel possessed a multitude of exceptional qualities as well. Among them, his capacity for intense listening and quick thinking, wherein he comprehensively considers all facets of a challenge, stands out. Additionally, his empathetic nature towards those experiencing difficulties is particularly noteworthy.

Dr Goel's contributions to the industry are vast and noteworthy, but one of his standout achievements has been pioneering the development of water-based lamination adhesives, which are tailored for automated high-speed lamination machines in India. This innovation addressed a critical need for Indian packaging producers, making the process both affordable and suitable for local environmental conditions. Earlier, he had also spearheaded the creation of ice water-resistant and polymer-based labelling adhesives, replacing the less efficient dextrin-based alternatives. The industry collectively rejoiced at the introduction of these brilliant Indian products, as they effectively resolved numerous production challenges and marked a significant advancement for all involved.

Dr Goel's book stands as a testament to his visionary leadership and his remarkable ability to turn his vision into reality despite time constraints. The fruits of his creativity and hard work are evident across his product line, which is widely appreciated by users globally. This book is a must-read for technologists, scientists, students, and aspiring entrepreneurs across the country who harbour dreams of achieving greatness. Dr Goel has painstakingly described how he transformed challenges into opportunities and entered the realm dominated by multinationals, effectively challenging them by developing indigenous Indian products. His narrative serves as an inspiration and a guide for those who dare to dream big and are willing to put in the effort to turn their aspirations into achievements.

This book is particularly invaluable for individuals seeking life lessons and practical guidance on entrepreneurship, especially for those aspiring to succeed as first-generation entrepreneurs. His story not only offers insights into overcoming obstacles and seizing opportunities but also provides a roadmap for navigating the challenges inherent in building a successful business from the ground up. Dr Goel's experiences and strategies serve as a beacon of hope and inspiration for those embarking on their entrepreneurial journey, offering invaluable lessons on resilience, innovation, academic brilliance, and perseverance.

Dr Goel's life is a testament to both the strength of the human spirit as well as the transformative power of entrepreneurship. In founding his own chemical company in 1990, he demonstrated remarkable foresight and entrepreneurial vision, navigating the complexities of business with the same precision and ingenuity that characterized his scientific endeavours. Yet, amidst the accolades and achievements, Dr Goel remained grounded in his values, guided by a profound sense of purpose and his commitment to making a positive impact on the world.

His dedication to environmental sustainability and social responsibility serves as a beacon of inspiration for future generations of innovators and entrepreneurs. His commitment to serving the academic community and institutions sets him apart.

As we embark on this literary odyssey through the life and times of Dr Goel, let us not only celebrate his remarkable achievements but also reflect on the lessons embedded within his life's journey. In this narrative, we find the quintessential embodiment of resilience, creativity, and the relentless pursuit of excellence. Furthermore, Dr Goel's story underscores the importance of interdisciplinary collaboration and the symbiotic relationship between academia and industry. His ability to seamlessly integrate scientific knowledge with practical application exemplifies the transformative potential that arises when diverse fields converge in pursuit of a common goal. It perfectly aligns with the 'Make in India' thought and imparts impetus to 'Viksit Bharat @2047'.

It is with great pleasure and pride that I recommend this memoir to readers far and wide, confident that Dr Goel's journey shall continue to inspire and resonate for years to come.

—Dr Rajendrakumar Anayath
Vice Chancellor of Maharshi Valmiki Sanskrit University, Kaithal, Haryana; Former Vice Chancellor of DCRUST

Preface

With faith in your own self, you can create your own destiny—this belief has shaped my life.

My life story has been an adventurous voyage of discoveries. At certain times, I felt like I had stumbled upon something new, but upon learning and reading a little more about it, I would realize that it already exists. During my childhood, my creativity took myriad forms—sometimes as a painter, at others as a writer or sculptor.

Today, at the age of 72, I continue to pursue these personal passions—I read something, think about it, and keep writing. I keep transforming. Back then, when my heart was filled with desire, I could etch out something beautiful. I did that by drawing lines or using a dash of colour.

Today, I have left my childhood behind.

My heart still longs to create and recreate through the medium of lines and colours. My destiny, and my work as a technocrat–entrepreneur, brought me closer to chemistry. However, the day-to-day management of business, with its routine tasks, left me with little time to pursue my passions, and creativity took a backseat. But through writing this memoir, I have been able to experiment with my creativity once again.

Now, I am bringing out my memoir at a time when the nation's youth are grappling with challenges in their personal and professional lives. The book you are holding in your hands, dear reader, isn't just any ordinary memoir. It can be read as a self-help book or an inspiring life story.

Historically, mankind has faced some challenge or another, even fought wars, to meet life's essential needs or to justify traditions

and religious beliefs. But in today's industrial age, most Indian citizens are fighting at two levels. The first struggle is to acquire an economic and technological edge, and the second is to strike a good work–life balance.

When it comes to industrialization, only a few developed nations have extended their sphere of influence in the entire world. In this situation, what does a developing nation like India, with 140 crore people, do? To become a developed nation, India must get the edge on industrialization and entrepreneurship. It has no other option. Can India lead the world in the sphere of industrialization and innovation? My answer is a resounding yes! In this book, I will attempt to illustrate this with the help of a few episodes from my journey. The two broad themes of this book are:

- How to set up a new business venture as a first-generation entrepreneur.
- How to lead a happy life by striking a good work–life balance.

If someone wants to start a business, how will they initiate it? How will they choose the product? How will the entrepreneur make a foray into a segment and proceed with limited resources? How will the person deal with government agencies, human resource issues, product selection, manufacturing, and marketing? This book will shine a light on all these aspects while striking a balance between work and life.

As I navigated the journey of life, I developed a few guiding principles. These are the principles that helped me set up my business and become a successful first-generation entrepreneur. In various chapters of the book, I will recount the ups and downs in my journey. Through this, I will explain how a person can manage to enrich their life with maturity and success despite all difficulties.

The policy of doing my work with complete honesty is something I inherited from my father, who was a teacher, and my grandfather, a leading educationist. It is a myth perpetuated over generations that to do business, you have to be dishonest. My story has always contradicted this myth! The success of Chemline—the company I founded and established in 1990—proves that if you conduct business with honesty, it pays off in the long run and you can move forward on the path of prosperity.

The other broad theme of my book relates to relationships. I will explain how one can fill the gaps in personal lives and relationships through the course of the book.

When I first began jogging my memory for my autobiography, I was not sure how many episodes of my life would be interesting and relevant for my readers. Even though I feel every stage of my life is important, my youth—when I chose to be an entrepreneur, the first in my family to do so—will form the nucleus of this book. I will elaborate upon how I judiciously converted the challenges I faced into life advantages.

An abiding credo in my life is: 'Don't just run after money. Focus on creating value and quality in whatever you do. Lead your life in a balanced manner. You must be stress-free and in the pink of health. Only then can you have a mind brimming with creativity and flowing with ideas.'

Upon experiencing any loss—whether personal, emotional, or material—people tend to slip into depression. I want to say that one must take these losses and convert them into strengths and opportunities. In my life, whenever such circumstances happened, whenever I missed somebody or lost something, I used it as a source of inspiration to create something much bigger; I did not brood over it.

During my college days at Delhi University (DU) and IIT, I used to paint and write poems. However, in the rat race of life, these passions continued to get suppressed. Over the years, in quieter moments, I used to think that I wanted to pursue more than just business and entrepreneurship and making money. I wanted to revive my creative instincts. But I couldn't pursue my dream because of one urgent business matter or another. For many years, I could not rekindle my creative pursuits. Finally, in 2023, my friend Alex helped kickstart this dream by arranging a meeting with Rupa Publications, who found my life experiences and entrepreneurial journey interesting and inspiring.

My story is a testimony to the power of perseverance. All of us have the divine inside us, so one should never feel helpless at any time. I believe the Almighty has sent me to this world with a specific mission. Whatever I have achieved, thanks to the Almighty, I want to dedicate to society and our nation. Through interesting anecdotes drawn from my eventful life journey, I hope my story can serve as an inspiration for young people and for generations to come.

Introduction
Moving Forward Is Life

My wife Sunita separated from me, with my son Kshitij and daughter Esha, in April 1989, after living together for nine years. After they left, I collapsed and had no strength. I was emotionally and financially broken. Various kinds of sicknesses engulfed me. The small adhesives factory, which I was running under the proprietorship of my wife, got shut down, and court cases were initiated. With a shock, life got entirely transformed!

Ek jhatke seh zindagi badal gayi, I thought then, my entire life suddenly changed so drastically. That is the beauty of life. It can offer so many colours, sounds, events, and experiences. What a wonderful life!

I left this traumatic experience behind and started building my life all over again through Chemline India Limited. I've lived thirty-five eventful years after I launched Chemline in 1990. So much has happened! What all didn't I do and experience?

The last thirty-five years I spent building Chemline are clearly alive in my mind. How did I start once again from scratch? My first manufacturing equipment was a *bhigona* or a kitchen pan, as can be seen below, with a capacity of around 100 kg, used to make curries or vegetables for get-togethers and parties. It was with this equipment, kept over bricks and firewood, that I started manufacturing labelling adhesives in the backyard of my house.

Processing glue in a bhigona or a huge kitchen pan

I travelled extensively across the country, and subsequently overseas, to sell this adhesive. I was like a man possessed—driven by a powerful emotion to rebuild my life. The impressions and memories of my travels are still vivid in my mind. Although I was travelling widely both within the country and outside, my children were always on my mind.

Life took another turn—this time, fuelled by passion. Despite many seemingly insurmountable hurdles, the process of winning started then and there. Today, I have created an industrial empire that started with a humble kitchen bhigona. Now I want to relive those experiences again and lead many more eventful years building and expanding Chemline to even greater heights!

I now live in an apartment and feel life in greater depth. I moved to this apartment about two months back (when I was writing this book), leaving behind my family and palatial villa, as I experienced a second separation after living together for over 30 years.

This second separation was another blow to my life. I could

not imagine living alone in an apartment, leaving behind my family. But there was no way out.

Although in the daytime, I was busy with business routines, the early mornings and evenings became lonely hours, filled with a disturbed mental state and sleepless nights. It took quite a few weeks to come out of this.

Once I overcame that state of mind, I started communicating with myself and thinking about the varied experiences that one gets in this lifetime. I chose to view these happenings positively, thinking, 'What a wonderful life this is, which gives you so much to experience.'

The new expansion process for Chemline has already begun. I want to create history in the coming years with the objective of making this company global and experiencing life through the process of business growth and other pursuits. Chemline already has customers across the globe in over 40 countries. I have once again initiated the process of creating novel products, technologies, and setting up manufacturing facilities for newer products.

Apart from all this, outside the sphere of my work, I have begun to explore myself through painting, writing poetry, practising music, and writing and sharing my experiences with younger generations. I want to experience more and more!

After having spent years of my life building this company, when I look back, I feel excited and overwhelmed by the experiences and impressions. This is what I want to share with my readers through this book. There is still so much to do and so much to achieve. Sometimes I think one lifetime isn't enough to experience everything that I desire.

My guiding philosophy of life is reflected in this poem that I wrote called 'Moving Forward Is Life' or 'चलना ही जीवन है'.

Keep moving, keep moving,
Moving forward is a goal,
Moving forward is life itself.

Do not stop in the face of difficulties,
Don't let any doubts creep into your mind.
Keep moving, keep moving.

The road may be difficult and monotonous,
But only by moving forward
Will you find peace, fame, and success.

Your caravan of fellow travellers will grow
As you continue on your journey
People will meet you and leave you along the way
But remember, my friend, my brother, you must not stop!

Keep flowing like a river,
Keep moving, keep moving.
Because life is all about moving forward,
Moving forward is a goal,
Moving forward is life itself.

चलते रहना, चलते रहना
चलना ही लक्ष्य है, चलना ही जीवन है|
कठिनाइयाँ देख कर न रुकना
मत रखना कोई संशय मन में||
चलते रहना, चलते रहना
चलना ही लक्ष्य है, चलना ही जीवन है

राह है कठिन...व नीरस...
परन्तु चल कर ही तो मिलेगा सुख चैन व यश|
चलते चलते काफिला बनेगा,
मिलने-बिछड़ने का यह क्रम चलता रहेगा,
मेरे बंधू, मेरे मीत, परन्तु रुकना न तुम|
नदी की तरह कल कल बहते रहना
चलते रहना, चलते रहना,
चलना ही लक्ष्य है, चलना ही जीवन है|

In the Upanishads, there is a phrase '*Charaiveti, Charaiveti* (चरैवेति चरैवेति)' which means 'keep moving forward'. In the face of every difficulty, I have adopted this as the central philosophy of my life. In fact, I often advise people to follow this approach in small steps. If you grow tired, pause for a while, regain your energy and then move forward again. Do not take a step backwards; instead take small steps every day to cover the long journey ahead. For example, when I began taking music lessons and painting at a late stage in my life, my friends were not sure about my objective. They said, 'What will you achieve by taking lessons once a month or once in 60 days?' I told them, 'Wait and watch. I will reply once I create a beautiful composition and painting one day.' I did attend classes once in 30 or 60 days, but I never altogether skipped my practice sessions.

I follow the same philosophy in my business journey as well. As the saying goes, an ocean is made up of small drops of water. Take a small step forward, but ensure that you make progress with each step.

PART I

My Story

1

Knowledge beyond Textbooks

I was born in the Nai Basti neighbourhood in Old Delhi (near Chandni Chowk) on 3 November 1953. I was the firstborn in a family engaged in serving Devi Saraswati, the goddess of learning. My grandfather, Lala Bishambhar Dayal, was an educationist who set up many government schools in the national capital. My father, Shri Satya Narayan Goel, was a teacher in DAV (Dayanand Anglo-Vedic) School and my mother, Smt. Daya Rani Goel, also joined the noble profession of teaching, albeit for a few years.

Within a couple of years of my birth, my joint family moved into quarters at the All India Institute of Medical Sciences (AIIMS) in South Delhi, after my uncle, Shri Bal Krishna Goel, who was a pathologist, was allotted official accommodation at the premier medical institute. My grandfather was then serving as a principal in one of the government schools in Sarojini Nagar. Soon after, I began my school education at the M.B. Primary School in Ansari Nagar, which was run by the municipal corporation. Later, when my uncle moved out of AIIMS, we shifted to a home in Yusuf Sarai, but my schooling continued at the same school.

One of my earliest memories from school is from the time I was in Class 1. My grandfather visited our school and met my headmaster to talk about my performance in studies, and they had a long conversation. After that conversation, they observed me in the classroom and from the next day, I was asked to attend Class 2. After studying in Class 1 for slightly more than a month, I had been promoted to Class 2! So I completed two classes in one academic year and had a head start over many other students.

I remember that our music teacher used to make the choir sing a song. I still remember the lyrics vividly: '*Naujawanon, Bharat ki taqdeer bana do; phoolon ke gulshan se kaanton ko hata do*, the youth of India, you must write the destiny of India; take out all the thorns from the blooming garden of flowers.' This was a song from the film *Kundan* (1955), imbued with patriotism for our motherland, and rendered beautifully by the inimitable Mohammed Rafi. A few years after Independence, the nation was brimming with optimism, idealism, and patriotic fervour, and our impressionable young minds were trained to reflect this. The credit for my interest in music goes to my mother, who was a really good singer. She was also an artist and passed on her interest in sketching and painting to me. She had a bachelor's in education and taught for a few years as well.

After completing Class 5 from M.B. Primary School, I moved to a government-run school in the Kidwai Nagar area for Classes 6 to 10. My mother's brother, my *mama*, Shri Hem Raj Gupta, who was an electrical engineer in CPWD, resided in Vinay Nagar, which was close by, and I had the opportunity to visit him frequently.

In Class 7, I developed a keen interest in solving mathematical riddles. Often, I would borrow magazines from a mobile library service (offered by the Delhi Public Library) and then spend hours solving the math riddles given on the last few pages of these magazines. These mobile libraries were a great boon to developing a reading habit among children from the middle class, particularly during the 60-day summer vacation. At a time when the incomes of government employees were too little to buy expensive books for their children, this was a great initiative.

At that time, I was confident that I had 'developed' a mathematical formula of my own. Say, you had to add up all the numerals from 1 to 100. The formula to solve this is $N \times (N+1)/2$. Let me illustrate this to the readers using the numerals 1 to 10. Consider N is 10. So, 10 multiplied by 11 (N+1) divided by 2 is equal to 55. If we add 1+2+3+4+5+6+7+8+9+10, that also equals 55.

Without any help from my teachers and my family, on the sheer dint of my creative brain, I had 'discovered' this formula in Class 7. In today's perspective, it is like writing software code! I was mighty pleased with myself and boasted to my classmates about this. My friends were amazed, and one of them asked me to demonstrate it to our maths teacher, whom we lovingly called Theta, as his round face and figure resembled the mathematical sign theta (θ). To my great disappointment, Theta was not impressed by my 'discovery'. He told me to sit down and said this formula was nothing new. When I studied further, I discovered there were a number of such formulae, but I had still come up with this on my own in Class 7.

Apart from academics, I also actively participated in physical exercises in the gymnasium, and I also loved to draw and sketch. I had inherited my creativity and painting skills from my mother, as mentioned previously. She was a creative soul. In the annual craft-modelling exam, she used to paint on clay figures of fruits for me and my younger brother, Mahendra, and they were greatly appreciated by my art teachers. Even my father encouraged me to further nurture my interest in art. On his bicycle, he used to take me to high-profile exhibitions in art galleries like the All India Fine Arts & Crafts Society near Connaught Place, to provide me with valuable exposure to art and artists during my early years.

Not just this, my father helped me get private art lessons from an artist who resided in Green Park. Although I was already decent at drawing, I learnt the fundamentals of drawing and painting from him for two to three months, thanks to my father's encouragement. He used to take private tuitions so that he could buy expensive textbooks and art materials for us. The discipline of working hard and not letting difficulties bog one down is something that I inherited from my father; this philosophy has always helped me.

If my mother inspired me with her creative faculties in singing and art, my father's hard work and practicality developed my personality in different ways. When I look at it, the two sides of my brain developed simultaneously and shaped my personality as a creative and successful chemical scientist and entrepreneur.

In 1968, my grandfather built a house in a neighbourhood called CC Colony, near Rana Pratap Bagh in North Delhi. Our family moved into this new home, as we were living in a joint family. I had to change my school from the Govt School in Kidwai Nagar to the Govt School in Shakti Nagar, North Delhi. While we were in South Delhi, when I was in Class 9, my mother's health deteriorated significantly. Her health problems meant that she could not pitch in with many household chores, such as cooking and cleaning. This meant that, as teenagers, my younger brother and I took up some of these responsibilities, and this affected my performance in Class 9. I continued my studies in South Delhi up to Class 10. For my Class 11, I enrolled at a school in Shakti Nagar, near CC Colony, where my grandfather had built his own house. This was also close to the North Campus of DU. In a way, destiny was already bringing me closer to my future college, right in the heart of DU!

In Class 11, I had to sit for exams conducted by the Central Board of Secondary Education.[1] A few months before that, my father realized that my level of preparation was not very high. Taking private tuition wasn't an affordable option for the family. Still, my father introduced me to some of his colleagues from school and asked them to assess my preparation in subjects such as English and Physics. His colleagues were of the opinion that I could make up for lost time quickly, provided I worked hard for three months. Going by this advice, I studied really hard for the next three months. I used to study throughout the night during those days.

---

[1]Before the Government instituted the 10+2+3 system in India in 1977, our country had four patterns of school leaving exams: 10+2+3, 10+2+2+2, 11+3, and 11–12+1+3. '1977-10+2+3 System of Education: The New Class Structure', *India Today*, 25 December 2009, https://tinyurl.com/2d5uhutb. Accessed on 13 May 2025.

I still remember the colony watchman calling out 'jaagte raho' during his night patrols.[2] I used to study till 5 a.m. every day before catching a few hours of sleep. In those days, securing a first division, or a score of 60 per cent, was really tough. The pattern of examination and evaluation was yet to shift to the regime of objective-type questions, and scores in the high 90s were uncommon.

On the day my results were out, I was sleeping on the terrace, under the stars. I still remember my father waking me up and announcing, 'Ravi, wake up and check your roll number in the newspaper. You have scored a first division in your results.' His voice was tinged with excitement and pride. He had good reason to be proud—his son was the only student in the neighbourhood to score a first division!

My father wasn't the only family member whose faith in me had been vindicated. My grandfather was mighty pleased, too. I remember he asked me to take out my bicycle and said, 'We have to visit somebody.' I wondered where he was taking me. I soon found out that my grandfather wanted to make a point to the principal of the Shakti Nagar school.

Mr Pathak, the principal, had initially been reluctant to give me admission to the school. 'It would spoil the results of my school,' he had argued. The school wanted students who could score a first class. Nevertheless, my grandfather had persuaded him to give me a chance. On that day, after his grandson had scored a first division, my grandfather proudly told the principal, 'Mr Pathak, at least now you can't say your school's results have been affected. My grandson has scored a first class and has made the entire school proud.' Mr Pathak was left with no option but to praise me and concede a point to my grandfather. This was just

[2]While this literally translates to 'stay awake', it is a common cultural phenomenon. Colony or neighbourhood watchmen shout out this phrase throughout the night to assure people that everything is okay. In some places, other sayings or even whistles are common.

the beginning of my academic journey, in which I went on to win a series of accolades.

In 1969, I enrolled for an honours degree in chemistry from Hansraj College in DU's North Campus. Now, reminiscing about my days in college, I remember the three years as a phase of intense academic rigour—an unending series of classes, tutorials and time spent reading in libraries. There was time for little else. The classes were mostly held in DU's Department of Chemistry, and we hardly spent time on the college campus at Hansraj. When I look back now, I realize there were hardly any extracurricular activities. There were few opportunities for students to display their talent outside their studies. Had I had more opportunities to go on the stage and display my latent talent for singing, I could have overcome stage anxiety and better developed my public-speaking skills.

The principal of Hansraj College at that time was the iconic mathematician Mr Shanti Narayan. He was a legendary academician, and the books penned by him on calculus were prescribed as textbooks in schools and colleges. Unfortunately, once I began pursuing chemistry, I paid little attention to other subjects. The passion for chemistry overtook everything else, including my first passion—mathematics and physics. Despite scoring a first class, I had not been able to get admission in physics.

Now that I had chosen to pursue the subject, I was consumed by the fundamentals of chemistry. My bond with the subject was becoming stronger with every passing day. Little did I know that it would take me to IIT Delhi and open doors for me to launch my own business, based on the fundamentals of chemistry. Although I didn't score very high marks in my college exams, I used to have quite a deep understanding of my subject. I appreciated the principles of chemistry and science from the roots. This stood me in good stead at crucial junctures of my life.

During this time, I used to commute from my home to college on a bicycle. Usually I would stay late at the University, reading books in the library and taking notes for my coursework as well. I used to return home and have dinner at 11 p.m.

▪

Right from my school days, I developed a conviction to look beyond conventional parameters of success and old definitions of learning. The first incident that shaped this belief was my earlier-mentioned encounter with the maths teacher, who did not recognize my initiative of developing a math equation on my own in Class 7. Instead of encouraging my proactive initiative, he dismissed it as routine. At that time, teachers were not appreciative of out-of-the-box initiatives by young students. Even now, I think that this continues to be a weakness of our education system that needs to change.

Over the years, as I made a name for myself in the discipline of chemistry and as an entrepreneur, I often wondered whether the best knowledge comes from conventional forms of education. Or whether one should seek knowledge beyond textbooks? There are several examples of entrepreneurs who went on to become the who's who of the business world despite dropping out of their courses.

One can find multiple instances of this trend, particularly in the world of start-ups and information technology. Bill Gates, for one, dropped out of Harvard to focus on Microsoft full-time. Facebook founder Mark Zuckerberg famously left university before relocating to Silicon Valley and the rest, as they say, is history. Closer to home in India, Dhirubhai Ambani—the pioneering founder of the Reliance Group—as well as Gautam Adani, did not complete their higher education. In fact, Dhirubhai did not even complete his schooling. Even Sadhguru Jagadish 'Jaggi' Vasudev of the Isha Foundation has often spoken about how he learned by looking beyond textbooks. Such unconventional paths to education do not mean one cannot make it big in their chosen profession or business.

In my own life, I've encountered several such instances. Had I just stuck to my textbooks and not developed my reading habit through mobile libraries and discovered the world of books, I would not have developed a belief in what I call 'freelance learning' or acquiring knowledge beyond textbooks. Right from school, throughout college and even during my doctoral studies, my passion for books and reading a variety of genres and authors continued.

My grandfather used to subscribe to a monthly religious Hindi magazine called *Kalyan*, published by Gita Press, Gorakhpur. They used to publish a series on the *Mahabharata*. My grandmother, Ram Bai, was fond of these stories, but her eyesight was weak, and she wasn't fluent in reading Hindi. So before I went to school in the afternoon shift, for close to two hours, I used to read out from the 11 hardbound volumes of the *Mahabharata*, published as a series in Kalyan, which we had at home, to my grandmother. In the process, I memorized all the incidents of *Mahabharata*, including the chapter in which the Pandavas go to Mansarovar.

During the two-month summer vacation in school, I used to complete my holiday homework in a single day and ask my father to allow me to read books and paint. In the process, I got introduced to global literary greats who wrote in Hindi, even though I was a school student myself.

Real knowledge comes from going beyond textbooks. I used to spend hours at DU's central library as well. It may not have resulted in higher grades, but it helped me widen my knowledge and in-depth understanding. This helped me perform well in every interview, as I was able to respond to every query thrown at me by every subject-matter expert. It was this knowledge, acquired from my wide-ranging reading habit, that helped me contribute articles and book reviews to the *Science Reporter*, one of India's oldest popular monthly science magazines.

Golden Days at IIT Delhi

Once I completed my MSc in chemistry in 1974, I was unemployed for close to a year. Public sector jobs were hard to come by. During this phase, I ran into one of my friends who was working at his father's rubber factory. He enquired about my employment status and future plans. Even without a job in hand, I was clear-headed and confident in my capabilities. I told him, 'Do you recall the Maxwell–Boltzmann Distribution Law? I understand it really well and also understand other important principles of chemistry. Since I understand the principles and their applications, I will find employment and get hired for a good position commensurate with my skills and be successful in life. So I am not unduly perturbed by not finding a job yet.'

In December 1974, I visited one of my uncles (mama), Shri Balraj Gupta, in Yamuna Nagar, Haryana. Armed with a master's degree in economics from St Stephen's College, he was the first entrepreneur in our extended family. He asked me to accompany him to a sugar mill there, as he knew the general manager and had introduced the two of us. The manager hired me immediately, and I got a job for a princely salary of ₹500.

I remember that the technical director and I used to argue a lot. He was related to the owner and wanted to enforce strict discipline on me, and I resisted. But even in my first job, I was brimming with ideas and creative ways to enhance the sugar yield and the factory's productivity. I worked in the mill till April 1975, when I spotted an advertisement in the *Hindustan Times*. This was the moment that would change my life.

I responded to the advertisement for a CSIR Fellowship at IIT Delhi. The posts were for a senior research fellow and a junior research fellow. I decided to apply for the fellowship, and did not work at the sugar mill for a few days. I took a written test, which was followed by an interview. One of the interviewers was the Director of the Shriram Institute for Industrial Research—an independent research institute conducting research and development (R&D) in areas of special significance to industry and government agencies. I successfully answered all the questions he asked and was granted on-the-spot admission. After the interview, one of the professors who had been on the panel told a PhD student, 'Ravindra is the only candidate to have answered all the questions correctly, and he has been selected.' This was later mentioned to me by that PhD student, once we became acquainted.

There is another interesting anecdote related to this. Initially, I was interviewed for inorganic chemistry. During the interview, I revealed my love for polymer chemistry to one of the professors. He gave me a tip-off and directed me to another venue in which interviews for polymer chemistry were being conducted. I requested Professor I.K. Verma to allow me to appear for the interview. She graciously agreed, and I answered all questions related to plastics and polymer chemistry. I got admission into IIT Delhi for a fellowship in material science and technology. This was a special moment in my life! I felt like I was on top of the world and immediately resigned from the sugar mill. It was a transition that changed my life and helped me become a polymer scientist, which ultimately paved the way for my entrepreneurial venture in adhesives.

I embarked upon my PhD studies in April 1975. My guides were Professor D.S. Verma of the Department of Textile Technology and his wife, Professor I.K. Verma, of the Department of Chemistry. The professor couple guided me for my thesis over the next three years. They had both done their PhD from Glasgow University. Studying at IIT Delhi changed my outlook towards the world of academics and widened my horizons. I got to understand the real purpose of education—it should not be about survival; rather, it should be about broadening your horizons. I have always believed so!

Initially, when I joined IIT Delhi, I used to spend two hours one-way to reach the campus from my home in Rana Pratap Bagh. But I didn't mind it, since I was really excited and happy about joining the elite institute. But after some time, I spoke to my father and decided to shift to the hostel on campus, as spending four hours every day in buses left me exhausted. My father agreed, and I became a hosteller soon.

■

Enrolling at the Vindhyachal Hostel at IIT Delhi in 1975 was a transformative point. The hostel was located close to the library and the laboratories, and I made the most of it.

Being a PhD scholar, you could work till late in the evening, conducting experiments in the labs. I loved the idea of working till late in the laboratories or enriching my knowledge of the subject by going through an array of journals and encyclopaedias, even if it meant sitting for hours altogether in the library. The IIT Delhi library was really nice. It had a wide selection of books and journals required for research. The overall atmosphere was ideal for me to hone my inherent inquisitiveness and develop it further. After 7 p.m., most day scholars returned home, and only a few dedicated students were around. Many times, I would return to the laboratory or library late in the night, after dinner at the hostel.

The campus was secluded from the noise and traffic of the city—it was lush, green, and quiet. There was absolutely no noise, and the setting felt nestled in the lap of nature, comprising manicured gardens and all-pervasive greenery. I just loved the atmosphere, as it was truly conducive to enhancing one's knowledge and applying its principles to develop practical solutions relevant to one's chosen academic discipline. The area was inhabited mostly by students and professors. There were hardly any vehicles on campus, and most residents walked down to the academic and residential areas.

The atmosphere at IIT Delhi motivated me to focus all my energies on my PhD programme. The subject of my research was high-temperature resistant polymers used in space research. That atmosphere nurtured learning and cross-pollination of ideas with discussions among all scholars, whether they were in the PhD or graduate programmes. Even at the hostel, you could make friends with talented people.

The campus also boasted excellent facilities for sports, including lawn tennis, badminton, and swimming. I loved to play badminton and swim very frequently. This atmosphere was a big departure from DU, where I had been a day scholar. The IIT Delhi campus was a special place. It was a compact unit, much larger, aesthetically designed, and with better facilities than the DU campus.

A few individuals helped nurture my passion for chemistry while studying at IIT Delhi. These included fellow students, peers and seniors. Lively discussions over the nuances of polymer chemistry, or any other topic under the sun, were part of everyday life on the campus. The faculty was excellent as well.

Apart from my guides, I used to interact with many other brilliant minds, some of the best in the world, who were part of the faculty at IIT Delhi. For instance, Professor M.L. Gulrajani, whose area of specialization was industrial and textile dyeing processes, motivated me to write and contribute articles in scholarly journals. He helped me publish a few papers in respected industry journals, which boosted my confidence as a contributing scholar and writer. Professor V.B. Gupta was another teacher I looked up to and have fond memories of from my days at IIT Delhi.

Unlike my days in DU, in which my potential for scientific research remained unfulfilled, I could realize it while studying at IIT Delhi. In DU, I was like a drop in the ocean and one among many students finding my way since student–teacher interaction was minimal. But at IIT Delhi, my interaction with the faculty enhanced to a great degree. This encouragement from my teachers helped me come into my own. An illustration of their confidence in my abilities was that, at times, teachers such as Dr I.K. Verma would direct students to me to help resolve their queries on the subject.

I garnered a lot of appreciation for my talent, wide knowledge, writing abilities, and academic rigour at this institute of learning. As a result, I finished my doctoral thesis in record time, in just two and a half years. By early 1978, I had completed my PhD at IIT, but I was not mentally prepared to leave the campus. I wanted to stay longer, as IIT Delhi had proved to be an ideal nursery for my research acumen and a cradle for knowledge. No wonder, I consider the days that I spent at IIT Delhi as the golden phase of my life, in which I could focus entirely on my passion for scientific research. I knew that once I moved out, I would miss its huge and spacious ambience, its library, its well-equipped laboratories, the walking tracks that took us to the hostel and, most of all, the cover of greenery laid out like a carpet all around the campus. But as it so happened, soon after completing my doctorate, I found a job at another premier Indian institute—AIIMS, not far from the IIT campus.

LIFE LESSONS

- Ensure you take small steps forward every day to cover the long journey of life. Don't take a step backwards.
- Hard work and perseverance can be accompanied by creative pursuits of your choice—whether art, music, or anything else you enjoy.
- Look beyond conventional parameters of success and keep learning to widen your horizons.

2

Entrepreneurship through Innovation

Right after completing my PhD in 1978, I had first sought a placement at AIIMS in New Delhi, as mentioned previously. I worked in the laboratory of Professor Madan Mohan, who was the ophthalmologist to the then president of India. He was interested in developing ophthalmic plastics. I worked in his lab for about six months. However, the doctors there looked down upon non-medical professionals. Realizing this deep-seated prejudice, I left AIIMS and joined Sir Padampat Research Centre (SPRC) at J.K. Synthetics in 1980.

I remember boarding the Dehradun Express from Delhi and getting off at Kota station. I spent three years at J.K. Synthetics in Kota. It was there that I got married and enjoyed family life with my wife and son. Although I was busy with work, my quest for innovation and creative ideas to enhance the productivity of the company continued like before.

At J.K. Synthetics, the company management asked me to research the usage of nylon waste. I put my heart and soul into researching the same. I studied de-polymerization, nylon polymerization, etc. While I was working there, I contributed half a dozen significant articles on nylon waste, after accumulating a world of wisdom on the subject from a wide range of published data.

Later, when I was leaving the company, these articles led to an interesting development, which included the chief engineer of the Projects and Development Department at J.K. Synthetics. For some time, I was involved in this department. When I resigned, I invited the chief engineer home for dinner. He then told me, 'Dr Goel, now that you are leaving JK Synthetics, I can reveal one thing to you.' I was intrigued. 'I am eager to listen to your revelation,' I told him.

He said, 'I was on a trip to Switzerland, as part of a six-member team led by the president of J.K. Synthetics. We went to visit the headquarters of Inventa, a Swiss company that had collaborated with J.K. Synthetics. We were in conversation with the head of R&D. We told the Swiss that we want to turn our nylon oligomer waste[3] into useful products through the process of depolymerization or further polymerization. No such technology with commercial application had yet been invented. Their head of R&D told us there is only one consultant who can help you achieve this—R.N. Goel. We realized that journals containing all six articles written by a Dr Goel were lying on his table. At this point, Mr Sitaram inghania, the president of J.K. Synthetics, enquired: "Who is Dr Goel? Where does Dr Goel stay in India?" He was informed that Dr Goel is an unsung researcher in our own R&D centre, namely, the Sir Padampat Research Centre, in Kota.' Mr Singhania never made the effort to come and recognize me. But I had the satisfaction of knowing what the chief engineer told me: 'The head of R&D at Inventa was reading your articles like a Bible!'

This incident is a reflection of an unfortunate trend in our society. We tend to put our blind faith in a Westerner, and do not encourage our own when they display proactive innovation and come up with brilliant solutions or demonstrate academic rigour and excellence. Unfortunately, in our society, many of us display a 'crab mentality' by trying to pull each other down. Had I been encouraged after the feedback received in Switzerland, it would have benefited the company immensely—I could even have

---

[3]During the process of nylon polymerization from caprolactam as the raw material, a 4 per cent oligomer by-product is formed.

been persuaded not to leave the company. In hindsight, this was a good incident, since it later inspired me to embark upon my own entrepreneurial journey.

After that, I got my next worthwhile job opportunity. I had responded to a newspaper advertisement and applied for a position at Indian Petrochemicals Corporation Limited (IPCL), based in Baroda (now Vadodara). During the interview, my PhD from IIT came in handy. I realized then that having an IIT qualification was a strong credential. This was a Government of India (GoI) undertaking, and I was offered the role of Senior Research Scientist. I joined in September 1982, just a few weeks before India showcased its economic prowess under Prime Minister Indira Gandhi at the Asian Games, commonly known as Asiad '82.

As India was coming into its own, I took the first step in my professional journey as a senior research scientist. It was a prestigious post! I got official accommodation in a township earmarked for IPCL employees. It was a leafy, sprawling neighbourhood with good facilities for sports, including a swimming pool. I remember that my wife and I had bought a Keltron colour TV worth ₹10,000 in Delhi and taken it to Baroda.

My job profile was directly associated with my passion for research. I began researching acrylic fibre—a subject I had already worked on in J.K. Synthetics. I consider my four-year stint at IPCL as the first big stride in my entrepreneurial journey. For the first time in my professional life, I was comfortable in my own skin. I was good at my work, eloquent and hardworking. My contemporaries often remarked that I was leaving a good impression on my colleagues and on everybody else that I interacted with.

One of those impressed with me was the IPCL chairperson Dr S. Ganguly. He wasn't a frequent visitor to the R&D department, which was a small non-profit arm of the public sector undertaking. Like my other colleagues, I too was keen to showcase the project that I was researching to the chairperson. My project was called 'Continuous Polymerization of Acrylonitrile into Polyacrylonitrile from where the Acrylic Fibre was made'. I told him that we would reduce the polymerization time to one-sixth of the current one—from 48 hours to 8 hours—thereby enhancing the productivity of the plant.

Mr Ganguly was really impressed with what I had promised. 'I see a lot of confidence in your eyes, Dr Goel. I am sure you will be able to achieve this,' he remarked. After that day, I got unprecedented access to the office of the chairperson. He began calling me directly in his room for advice on research projects. Even as I became the cynosure of his eyes, a wave of envy and jealousy gripped my colleagues, including the person in charge of the department. But Dr S. Ganguly was a man of science, and he saw a spark in me and continued to encourage me. This did wonders for my self-esteem and confidence, and that in turn went on to open new doors for me. My creativity and imagination began to soar, and so did my worldview.

Even my first visit abroad in 1984, to New York in the United States (US), happened when I was at IPCL. We wanted to set up a pilot plant for acrylic polymerization and visited the US for negotiations in this regard with a project management consultant. Technology wasn't very developed in the country back then, and technical know-how was mostly imported. Therefore, the purpose of the visit was to acquire technical knowledge for the team members, many of whom were really young.

The flight to New York marked my first time travelling abroad, and that too, in first class. The GoI ensured that its senior R&D scientists travelled in style! The food was delicious, and we reached New York late in the evening. One of my distant relatives was at the airport to receive me. At the time, most government officials didn't want to spend much on hotel stays and instead preferred to lodge with their relatives. I did the same while in New York.

When the Chairman, Dr Ganguly, heard I was travelling to the US, he passed on a gift to me to be handed over to his sister in New York. It was the good old *gur* (jaggery), but prepared in the Bengali style with palm dates. Once we reached New York, I realized I had no way to visit her since I didn't have a car and there was no easy public transport option available! I was left with no option but to send her the package through post.

From New York, we went to Florida and stayed in a hotel there. On the way back, we stopped at Bonn (in Germany) to visit M/s Fourne, a company which specialized in setting up pilot plants for making synthetic fibres such as nylon and acrylic. We came back to India and reached Vadodara via Bombay (now Mumbai). It was on the day that Indira Gandhi was assassinated that I took an early morning train to Vadodara. As we left Delhi behind, riots began raging, but I was fortunately out of harm's way and reached Vadodara safely.

Milestones

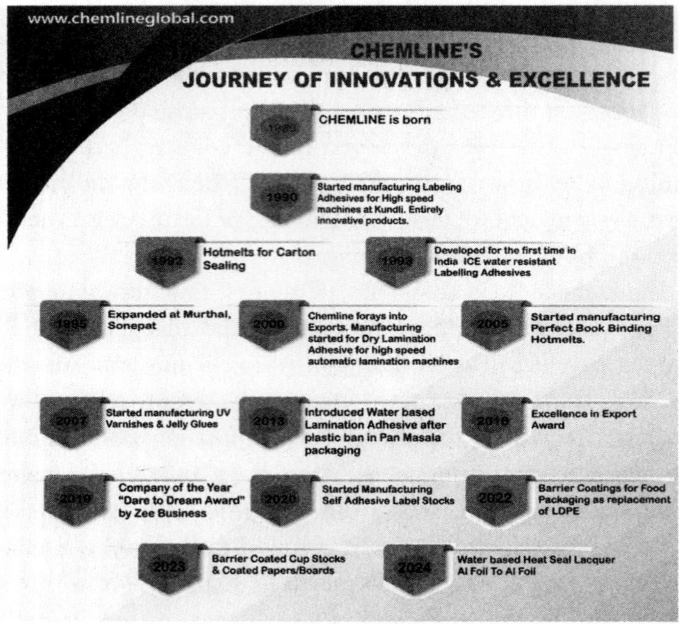

What Chemline Is Today

Our never-ending quest for innovation and growth has continued unabated. Over the years, we have expanded into multiple industrial verticals and added a wide range of products. Today, Chemline is a leading Indian company manufacturing over 500 adhesives, coatings, papers, and other downstream products for diverse industrial applications, exporting to more than 40 countries worldwide.

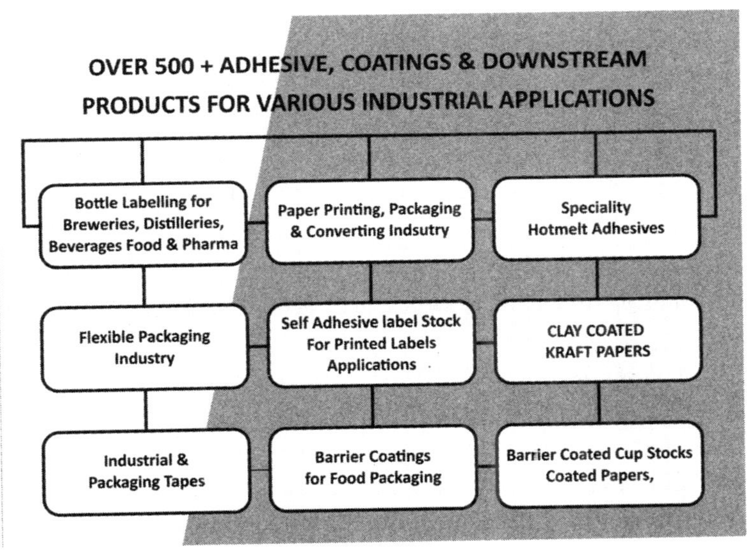

Chemline offers a diverse range of products across various industries

All these products are manufactured at a single location spread across 12 acres of land. The facility houses separate, state-of-the-art manufacturing plants with HiTec systems dedicated to each product line. The campus is fully equipped with modern research and development laboratories staffed by highly qualified and experienced scientists. Separate and equally advanced laboratories are dedicated to quality control, product application, and testing. Approximately 300 trained and skilled professionals work at Chemline today.

Creating a Unified Voice in the Industry

Running an industry in India in those days was not easy, as there was a great deal of red tape. As far as government authorities were concerned, they viewed us as milch cows—a source of endless income through illegal extortion. Let me illustrate this through an example. Despite my keenness to pay taxes, when I applied for a sales tax number, I only got it after an excruciating period of six months. They made me run from pillar to post before allotting me a sales tax number. Such was the extent of red tape in the government. Getting credit to launch your business was not easy. Applying for a loan from the banks or the Haryana Financial Corporation involved being buried under a mountain of paperwork and filling out countless forms. It must have taken me more than seven months to get a loan of about ₹7 lakh. I made numerous visits to Chandigarh to meet government officials, having secured appointments, only to find that they were absent on the scheduled day, offering flimsy excuses. It was really frustrating to see the apathetic attitude of government servants at the time.

To fight the infamous licence raj of the government, before liberalization gained momentum in the early 1990s, was difficult. To overcome this obstacle, I first thought of unifying various stakeholders in the industry and creating an industry body. There used to be an existing industry association in Kundli, and I joined it as an executive member. Subsequently, they realized that I was very articulate and good with drafting letters and applications addressed to the government and decision-makers. They realized that I had the power to convince people with rational arguments and knew how to deal with inspectors, supervisors and other government officials. They immediately decided to appoint me as the general secretary of the association.

It was the onset of industrialization in the country in 1991, and the government was gradually cutting some of the red tape at the Centre, but it was yet to percolate down to state governments.

The finance minister of the country was Dr Manmohan Singh, and the prime minister was P.V. Narasimha Rao. These two were the architects of India's shift from a socialist economy to a free-market liberalized economy. The association president, myself, and other active members ensured that we took the voices of the stakeholders to the government. We streamlined our relationship with various government departments, such as Industry, Excise, and Sales Tax departments, to impress upon them the problems of entrepreneurs. We also asserted that they should not perceive us as cash cows to be extorted.

They realized our point of view, and this helped us overcome many roadblocks. Along with making our case with various heads of departments, I used to write to the state chief minister very frequently and apprise him of the situation on the ground and of the level of corruption that we had to encounter on an almost everyday basis. This led to a situation that every time Mr Om Prakash Chautala, the then chief minister, stopped at Kundli—on his way to some other destination—he would meet us and have a cup of tea with the association members. Even today, I can look back at my work with the Kundli Industrial Association with satisfaction.

After an initial success at the Kundli Industrial Area, I needed more land for expanding my factory, and acquired 2 acres in 1995 to build a factory in Dhaturi, near Murthal in the Sonipat district. It was a piece of agricultural land that was more economical compared to the government's industrial plots. It was bang in the middle of the countryside and next to a village. Since it was a large piece of land, we began building a boundary wall around it. This brought in its own share of problems. A few mischief makers from the adjoining areas began bothering us. They said, 'Fine, you are building this big factory here. What's in it for us? What will we get?' A few local goons began to threaten us.

Once the calls became a little too frequent for my comfort, I went directly to the Superintendent of Police (SP). I explained the problem to him, saying, 'I have launched a factory in the village.

It is providing employment to a lot of people there but I am still getting threatening calls. They want to extort money from me through intimidation.' The SP was of immense help. On the basis of the details I had provided, including the number used to make threatening calls, the police tracked the perpetrator. Overcoming these problems was part of the teething issues in the new premises.

As our factory was located in a remote area without any other industrial units around the village, ensuring safety and security was paramount. To this end, I hired a gunman at the factory along with two guard dogs—an Alsatian and a German Shepherd. When I visited the factory, I had to cross a 1-km desolate stretch before reaching the Grand Trunk Road. The gunman would drop me off at the Grand Trunk Road.

After the incident involving threatening calls, I became even more conscious of the need to keep my business secure. I came from a working-class and literate background. At first, I did not know how to react to these threats, as I had never faced such a situation before. The solution to this problem came with the formation of an industry association that I had envisaged. Its roots lie in the Kundli Industrial Association, as mentioned earlier. Apart from the personal security measures, I brought together the proprietors and managers of all the companies located along the Grand Trunk Road. Naturally, they appreciated the initiative. We kept in constant touch with local authorities, including the SP and the Deputy Commissioner of the Sonipat district administration.

This episode taught me a valuable lesson: Apart from yourself, you have to work for the welfare of the entire industry as well. We helped them find solutions to every problem with the creation of a very strong industry association called the Dhaturi Industrial Association. As the founder-president, I used to write letters to the chief minister, highlighting these issues. Whether it was applying for a telephone connection or power supply, everything was caught in the red tape. One had to activate the Telecom, Electricity, and Labour departments by writing to them. Also, one had to fight the excesses of the Excise and Sales Tax department officials. Running an industry was such a tough proposition during those days.

Gradually, the Dhaturi Industrial Association began gaining popularity and appreciation. At this time, the industrial corridors of Haryana were in the initial stages of being developed. The government, along with the HSIIDC, encouraged entrepreneurs and even assigned them plots of land for industrial use. As an industry association president, I was invited to events inaugurated by the HSIIDC. Part of our popularity with the authorities was because of our credibility. We had worked hard to build a reputation of honesty and credibility with our tireless efforts against corruption. In both the Kundli and Sonipat industrial areas, new businesses and entrepreneurs faced a common plight—arbitrary raids and harassment by excise and sales tax officials.

Let me recount an incident here. A young manager of a large factory in Kundli once approached me and said, 'Dr Saheb, I have heard a lot about you and need your help. Recently, we were raided by the excise department officials. They did not allow our staff to leave for the entire night. We are facing a lot of harassment from the officials. They seized our documents and took away all our books of accounts.'

I advised him to meet the Deputy Commissioner of Excise. I called up the concerned official and informed him of the harassment. 'Don't worry, Dr Goel, we will return the books of accounts,' said the official. I was glad that I could be of some help to another entrepreneur who was being unnecessarily harassed by the authorities. These were remnants of what was once the infamous licence raj.

Soon, word spread that Dr Goel does not hesitate to take on corrupt officials who are trying to harass entrepreneurs. A few days later, I realized that even the authorities had got wind of this. On that very day, I spotted an inspector visiting a factory that was located near our plant in Kundli. I told the Kundli Industries Association vice president, Subhash Gupta, that we must enquire whether our neighbour was being harassed by the inspector.

On reaching the plant, our fears came true. The inspector was comfortably perched with pockets full of money that he had extorted from the entrepreneur. He had packs of currency notes in his hands, which he was counting. He immediately recognized us and realized he had been caught with his hands in the till. He became anxious, and we asked him to empty all his pockets and return the ill-gotten money to the entrepreneur. We then asked him to escort us to our factory, where he apologized to us and said that he wouldn't harass entrepreneurs again.

Such was the impact of our efforts as an industry body. Through our relentless work, I can look back with satisfaction and say, 'Yes, we helped cut through the red tape and did our bit to challenge the notorious licence raj, which was a far cry from the ease of doing business nowadays.'

One day, Yudhvir Singh Malik, the then managing director of the HSIIDC, visited our office at the Kundli Industries Association for an event, in which I, as the general secretary, was the main speaker. After the event, the gentleman remarked:

> It is the first time that I am returning from an industry event having learnt a few new facts and deep insights. It is a big departure from other events. Wherever I go, the conversation does not move beyond a garland welcome, snacks, and felicitation. It is to the credit of the KIA and its dynamic president and general secretary, Dr Ravindra Goel, that I am returning home with new insights into how industries function and the challenges that entrepreneurs face while setting up a new business and keeping it going. Some of the aspects of the kind of policy measures and support systems expected from the government bodies to encourage local industries were also discussed during the meeting. Now that we understand your problems and expectations, we will work towards resolving them at the level of the HSIDC (now HSIIDC).

It is this ethos and legacy that we carried forward with the Dhaturi

Industries Association, which was formed at the new premises since the factory was located in Village Dhaturi. We continued to build on the foundation we had laid, as a vocal and dynamic industry forum that did not hesitate to engage with the government and policymakers on the issues faced by young entrepreneurs, particularly the excesses of the licence raj. We gave voice to the industry's problems and protected its interests to sustain growth.

Endings and Beginnings

परिवर्तन

मैं एक मोड़ पर से निकला
और गुज़र गया।
एकाएक देखा मैंने उस मोड़ को।

एक सीधी लंबी सड़क...
बहुत देर से इस सड़क पर
चलता आ रहा था,
और मोड़
इतनी जल्दी आ पहुंचेगा,
मुझे इसका एहसास तक न था

एकाएक...
जब मैंने मोड़ को देखा तो
चौकन्ना सा हो गया।

जैसे मोह हो गया था मुझे सीधी सड़क से,
अब मुड़ने का मन नहीं कर रहा था,
रह-रह कर दिल पिघल रहा था।

मोड़ के पश्चात,
फिर दूर तक सीधी नज़र आती सड़क
और, सड़क से शाखाओं सी निकली राहें
जो कुछ दूर जा कर कहीं खो जाती।

आस-पास, इधर-उधर देखने पर भी,
कोई नहीं दिखता,
सो मैं कुछ समय के लिए वहीं बैठ गया,
मैं किसी के मिलने की आशा कर रहा था।

मैंने पीछे मुड़कर देखा,
मैं बहुत दूर तक सीधा ही चला आया था,
पीछे की उबड़-खाबड़ राह, छूट चुकी थी,
अब, बिलकुल समतल दिख रही थी।
परन्तु अब मैं मुड़ चुका था एक नयी राह की ओर
यह नयी राह भी मुझे
अत्यंत सुन्दर प्रतीत हो रही थी।

Transformation

I came off a turning on the road
And walked away.

Startled, I glanced behind—

A long, straight road I could find
For quite some time,
On this road
I had walked in monotone,
And this curve
Had approached so suddenly
I barely realized

Watching that turn,
Still surprised,
Regained my composure, I became cautious
Walking on that straight road, fascinated me.
My heart was melting every now and then
I didn't want any twist

But after turning,

It looked like a long straight road,
Though it branched off into small walkways
Going a little farther, these walkways became invisible.

Around, looking around,
No one is visible.
So I sat there for a while,
I was hoping to meet someone.
I looked behind—
I'd come on a long, straight road.
The rough road behind was gone,
Now, it looked plain

But now I'd turned
Onto a new road
And this new road—
was looking very pleasant.

आनंद का परिवर्तन

भर लो स्वयं को परिवर्तन से इतना,
कि, खत्म न हो पाए यह परिवर्तन
उन्मुक्तता का,आनंद का,
कभी न ख़त्म होने वाली अनुभूति का
स्पंदन है इस परिवर्तन में।

परिवर्तन, जो शास्वत नियम है
प्रकृति का इसमें है सहज आनंद|
तो आओ स्वयं को जी लो मन से,
भर लो इस जीवन को परिवर्तन से||

The Transformation of Joy
Fill yourself with transformation,
Immerse yourself so deep that
the transformation becomes never-ending—
a transformation of joy,
of happiness and spontaneity
This transformation brings with it
a beautiful feeling
Of never-ending, eternal joy.

So, enjoy the transformation spontaneously
for it is an eternal rule of nature.
Celebrate yourself
and do what your heart desires,
Fill this life with change,
with transformation.

Situations and circumstances are changing, people around us are changing, and the whole world is changing. So one must always be prepared for change. Rest assured, change will keep happening, and life will continue in this manner. Change is the only constant in life! To remain happy, one must always welcome, relish, and appreciate change. Keep adapting and enjoy the changes that circumstances bring to you.

■

During my time at IPCL, they once sent us to Pune for a workshop on management. The consultant was a really innovative person. He introduced us to achieving results through the analysis of dreams. After an exhaustive meditation session, he asked us to write down our biggest dream on a sheet of paper and to keep the sheet below our pillow before sleeping. This exercise led me to finding an answer to a question that had been on my mind for many years: 'Should I continue working at IPCL or leave and launch my own business?' That was my biggest dilemma. I wrote down my dream and concentrated on the thought before sleeping. That very night, I had a dream in which I got my answer! The universe showed me the way. I decided to be the master of my own fortune and launch my own business.

Now that my entrepreneurial dreams had been sparked, fate was taking me closer to launching my own business venture. My mama, Balraj Gupta, was the founder of Polyplastics. He approached me to help him with his business, wherein he had a number of business partners and a complex ownership structure. He wanted me to work with his son Kamal Gupta

and created a joint venture for the two of us. My uncle said that he would make the investment for the business and that we would work in an equal partnership. We thought of beginning with the business of adhesives, since it can be launched with limited resources and does not require investment on a large scale. I agreed on the condition that I would share 25 per cent of my own share with my younger brother, Mahendra Nath Goel. We named our business venture Macro Vinyl. The year was 1986.

IPCL wanted to foster the spirit of taking risks and entrepreneurship in its employees, and even gave six months' leave to pursue ideas in entrepreneurship under their Entrepreneurship Development Scheme. Under this scheme, I applied for a six-month leave, and the Macro Vinyl venture was off the ground and running. Unfortunately, IPCL did not approve my application.

Around the same time, I had applied for a vehicle loan from

the company and bought a Maruti 800 worth ₹82,000, which had been approved. Despite my application for six months leave not being approved, and even with the car loan, I had made up my mind to leave the company, and the management had also decided that we must part ways. Dr Ganguly asked me about the car loan, and I promised him that I would return every single penny I had borrowed from the company.

Now, I wanted to be an entrepreneur. So I joined my maiden venture full-time in 1987. My brother, Mahendra, who was employed with Blue Star, could not devote much time to the business. Before I left IPCL, I couldn't come on board full-time either. Despite the time constraints, I knew we had hit upon a winning formula, literally. I had come up with the formulation technology. The adhesive that we manufactured was flying off the shelves! We had no unsold products and were finding it difficult to meet the demand.

The idea of a pressure-sensitive adhesive that is used to make stickers was a very sound one. It was an idea whose time had come. However, as mentioned earlier, Mahendra was unable to give the business his complete attention. Gradually, my uncle's interest in the Macro Vinyl venture also began to diminish, as he had parted ways with his business partners and had decided to get his son Kamal on board with his business. So he said he wanted to be excused from the Macro Vinyl venture, and in turn wanted us to return the investment he had put in. At this point, I asked Mahendra to come on board full-time. However, he could not do that.

For all these reasons, the business venture for pressure-sensitive adhesives did not flourish further. My brother, I, and my uncle decided to amicably part ways. However, there was an additional problem—my share was in the name of my wife. Even as the business had improved, my relations with my wife had begun to deteriorate. The distance between us widened since I spent most of my time in Delhi, trying to make the business grow, while she was in Vadodara. This led to emotional differences as well. Moreover, she had seen her side of the family suffer after the entrepreneurship bug had bitten her father. My father-in-law had left his secure employment and started a business that did not run smoothly. So my wife and her father were against me starting my own business.

In October 1988, my wife Sunita moved out of our home. Once she left, it created problems in the business, as she was the signing authority for all financial transactions, including banking, being the proprietor of the company. All this time, while I had focused on the technical and production side, she had managed the finances and paperwork. I was not just dealing with a personal setback, even our business venture had also become untenable! Legally, I could no longer visit the factory, as the ownership was in her name. My lawyer advised me against doing so while we were in the process of separating. Looking back, this may not have been the best advice. I should have continued business operations under my own name instead. It was an extremely challenging time for me, both professionally and personally. This unfortunate situation marked one of the lowest phases of my life.

I was dealing with a serious personal loss while also trying to look at the bigger picture. I realized I had liabilities to the tune of ₹10 lakh, which appeared to be an insurmountable burden. Payments were due to suppliers and other creditors. Ultimately, I had to close down the Macro Vinyl venture.

I knew I had to pull myself out of this abyss. But at that time, the injury was fresh. After my wife left, for the next nine months, I struggled with anxiety and depression. I had lost my appetite and my sleep, and had dark circles below my eyes. I consulted mental health practitioners and a psychiatrist as well, to no avail. During this phase, one day, I visited my uncle at Batra Hospital, and he recommended that I spend some time at the Sri Aurobindo Ashram in South Delhi. I spent a few hours in their prayer rooms and library, and renewed my relationship with reading. I read the writings of acclaimed spiritual leader and philosopher Sri Aurobindo. The philosophies of Swami Vivekananda and Sri Aurobindo left a deep impact on me.

At the Ashram, I met an Indian–American healer who was offering acupressure lessons to everybody completely gratis. He demonstrated an acupressure technique and then asked me to do it myself at home twice a day. On that day, it was as if a load had been lifted off me. I no longer felt like an insomniac. I experienced immediate relief and visited my uncle Shri Bal Krishna Goel's home, where I promptly fell asleep. I didn't even wake up in time for lunch that afternoon. When I did wake, I realized I was hungry for the first time in many months. My loss of appetite had also disappeared. For me, a small piece of advice from an alternative healer had managed to achieve what months of medication and guidance from mental health practitioners had not.

Over the next few weeks, I was back on track and on the road to recovery. It had been a turbulent few months—I missed my family, in particular, my children.

After regaining my appetite and beating insomnia, I knew I had to make a fresh start. I was heavily in debt. I took a vow that I would no longer remain sick or depressed, and I visualized a beautiful future waiting for me. I further imagined myself evolving into a renowned industrialist. In my own thought process, I clearly saw myself becoming an entrepreneur. I still remember the date—it was 25 December 1989. I wrote this briefly in my diary in Hindi, which I used to maintain before sleeping at night: 'Mujhe ek badi company ka malik banna hai; I want to become the owner of a large company.'

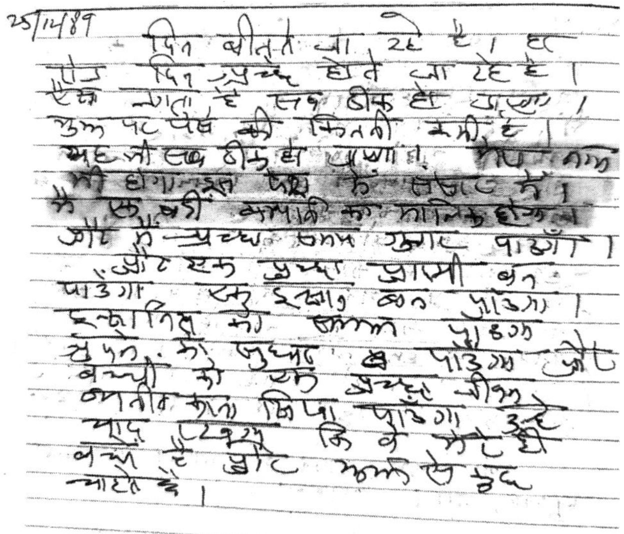

Visualizing my transformation as an industrialist through self-reflection

I made this visualization after I had begun recovering from an illness that had lasted eight months. At that time, I had no source of income. My two children and my wife, whom I deeply loved, had left me eight months earlier. I was burdened with a loan of ₹10 lakh. After writing this in my diary, I went to sleep that night with renewed resolve. Indeed, with such positive self-affirmation, I began to work on myself.

Soon after, I began thinking seriously about what product I should manufacture, and I started working earnestly on product development. After several months of hard work in my makeshift kitchen laboratory at home, I developed a product made from industrial waste—a labelling adhesive suitable for glass bottles. The raw material was sourced from IPCL at a negligible cost. The production cost was minimal, while the product fetched up to ₹85 per kg.

The initial commercial production was carried out in a 100-kg kitchen bhigona, as shown earlier. My first customer was Nestlé

India Ltd, which used the adhesive for labelling Maggi ketchup bottles. This success led to many more prestigious clients, including United Breweries for beer bottle labelling, Radico Khaitan for whisky bottles, and Hamdard Wakf Laboratories for labelling the iconic Rooh Afza bottles.

After an initial start using a kitchen bhigona, production was shifted to the first makeshift motorized mixer, as shown below.

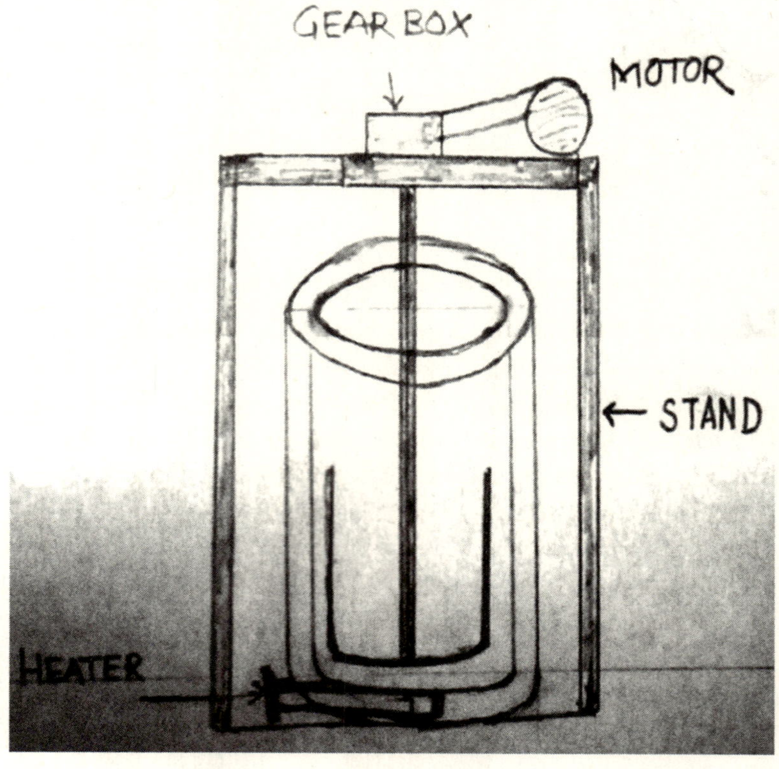

First makeshift motorized mixer with an 80-litre capacity

Now, I give others the same advice: 'Speak to yourself, write down your thoughts in a journal, and truly believe in them. It helps strengthen your subconscious mind.' This positive affirmation steadily brings clarity and offers guidance in selecting a future path. Taking this step helped me declutter my thoughts and move forward. I told myself, 'It's alright that you don't have anything today. You have liabilities of ₹10 lakh to various creditors, but you'll be a great entrepreneur one day.' I made this resolve at the age of 36.

CONTECH ADHESIVES INTL.
~~CHEMTEC~~
PLASTI-LINE
AdChem
Almac
4. Ameron
5 Chemtrol
6. Comco
7. Contech / POLYTECH
8 Du Pont
9. Ionac
10. Key Polymer
11 Loctite
12 Permacel
13 POLYCAST
14 ARVIN.
ArChem
CHEMLINE
HIGH POLYMERS
CHEM
TECH
POLY
AD.
PLAST
CAST
ACRY
LINE
CHEM CON
CHEM LINE
CHEM CENTRAL
ADLINE
Ariandee
TechLINE
POINT
Do CHEM
SUNCHEM

Brainstorming ideas for the company's name

The next night, I once again sat with myself and began writing in my diary. Wrapped in a quilt to ward off the biting December cold, I gave thought to what the name of my company should be, which will make it stand out in the industry. I created two columns on the page and wrote 10 names under each. I considered both columns side by side, hoping to come up with a unique name based on an amalgamation of the terms. Beginning with words like 'chemistry', 'polymer', and similar terms, I arrived at a combination of 'chemistry' and 'line'. After toying with the idea of 'Chemi-line', I finally decided to name my venture 'Chemline'. That's how the Chemline Group got its name.

By the grace of God, I formally launched Chemline in April 1990 and thus began my new journey towards success! Although my personal life was falling apart, I had to piece it together through a venture in adhesives. My entrepreneurial journey started in the Kundli Industrial Area. At that time, I had a piece of land, but little else.

I had applied for an industrial plot with the Haryana State Industrial & Infrastructure Development Corporation (HSIIDC; previously Haryana State Industrial Development Corporation [HSIDC]) by depositing ₹10,000. I had borrowed this amount from one of my elderly neighbours, Shri Ram Kumar, whom I addressed as uncle. A few months later, after an interview, my application was accepted, and I was asked to deposit a further ₹14,000 to secure the allotment of a 1,000 sq. m. plot. Once again, I borrowed this money from Shri Ram Kumar. He never asked for the money back, as he said that this money was auspicious for me. I kept on paying 2 per cent monthly interest to him. After his death, I have paid the interest amount to his daughter-in-law, as per his desire. Additionally, I took loan of ₹80,000 from a friend of my father, whom I used to call *chacha ji*. Both these uncles always admired me and had confidence in me; they gave me money without even consulting my father. The ₹80,000 was used to build a boundary wall and two small rooms, one to serve as a store room and the other for the factory's security guard, who also doubled up as a worker.

This was the only funding I had. I bought everything with this money, including waste raw materials and bhigona. At that time, even to make a telephone call, one had to visit the state border and use a public telephone booth. This was the only way to inform our clients that their product was ready and would be delivered soon.

Never a Dull Day as an Entrepreneur

In my view, entrepreneurship provides you with a unique perspective towards life. This perspective is very different from what other professions can hope to provide. Every day in the life of an entrepreneur brings forth new challenges, ensuring that no two days are the same. You can never complain of monotony or predictability. You go to sleep thinking that the next day you will have to wake up and solve a particular challenge. No two challenges have an identical solution. It challenges you to hone your skills in diverse disciplines, such as human resource development, finance, marketing, developing government relations, and technical excellence, and anticipating future trends of technology and market demand. Very few careers can boast of providing all these opportunities.

Also, when you think you are having a dull day, a fresh challenge will emerge out of nowhere and force you to think on your feet and shed your lethargy. A call may suddenly come about a new challenge—it could be about your business losing money, a customerproviding you with a problem, or a product not working.

You may have to fly in and resolve the issue, or you may have to motivate your team to reach the site when the team member may be reluctant to work on an off day or because of a family engagement. You might have to persuade the team member to put the organization first, in the interest of the business, and not lose a client.

Such challenges appear even at the smallest level. Say, for example, a vegetable vendor selling tomatoes from a handcart. He may have borrowed money from a lender to buy the tomatoes he wants to sell that day. Given our chaotic traffic conditions, it is likely that a vehicle could hit his cart. The cart might overturn, and all his tomatoes could end up squashed on the road. However, he still has to pay back the loan he had taken from the moneylender. An entrepreneur like him has to take on higher levels of risk and overcome day-to-day challenges.

Here's another example—let's say you have developed a unique product that is, to an extent, process-driven. In the highly competitive market that India is today, the competitors are desperate to discover a line of business and/or products that have the potential to challenge your current status. Within the first few years, a lot of competitors are likely to enter that space. The entrepreneur is once again compelled to think about a few questions, such as: How to reduce production costs? How to sustain the market share? How to keep new competitors at bay?

One day, you may think that sustainable food packaging is a new area for you to venture into with the potential of making profits. However, within two years, you will find that 15 new competitors have entered the same space. You will see that they haven't just displayed a herd mentality, but that they have also stolen your technology and poached some of your talented colleagues.

In such situations, you will suddenly realize that you are left with no resourceful people. When building a team, you will need to keep your flock together and also build an alternative set of people ready to take over, in case someone gets poached.

You must treat your colleagues like family and build a bond with your team members. Trust your employees the way you would trust your own family, and make them feel like they are part of a larger corporate family. Only then will you develop a personal connection with them. This, in turn, will pave the way for them to begin taking ownership of their actions and treating their workplace as their own company—that is the kind of loyalty an entrepreneur must work towards creating. No business venture can flourish, or attract and retain good people unless it develops a reputation as a good workplace with an empathetic employer.

Therefore, harnessing human capital through good leadership and developing positive relationships with colleagues and employees can work wonders in the success story of an entrepreneur. Of equal importance are trademarks and patents, which will ensure that your innovations and research are protected from theft by your competitors. The onus of ensuring that their patented technology is not misused by others is also on the entrepreneur. These are just a few of the challenges that keep entrepreneurs on their toes at all times.

At the beginning of my entrepreneurial journey, I wore a number of hats. Not only did I develop the technology needed for the Chemline business model, but I was also involved in scaling the business. I donned the hat of a chemical engineer to design the process plant and devise a system for the progress of the business. This was followed by designing a building for the factory, which involved acquiring knowledge of building materials and architecture. Subsequently, you have to create awareness about your product in the market and display your marketing skills.

Another useful trait for an entrepreneur is flexibility of the mind. You cannot hope to build a business with a rigid mindset. Unless the entrepreneur reinvents the business and the technology, they cannot stay relevant. Not only do you need to stay ahead of the technology curve, but you must also be on guard against copycats who want to imitate your successful products.

In a nutshell, an entrepreneur must be an active and alert person who is also very creative, as he grapples with new challenges every single day. This makes an entrepreneur's life really interesting. Therefore, I would urge young people to aspire to have such a career. Initially, there might be a few difficulties that appear insurmountable. But gradually, as you go along, it becomes an interesting life to lead.

In my case, I come from a family of teachers and educationists. Nobody else in my immediate family had ventured into entrepreneurship before me. Still, I chose to pursue what my heart and mind were telling me. I went ahead and capitalized on my knowledge of science, polymers in particular, to launch Chemline. The days when I did not have even seed capital for my business venture were not easy. But a realization dawned on me that I was destined to become a high-profile business entrepreneur.

My advice to fellow first-generation entrepreneurs is that you should start on a small scale, with a business that does not need a large capital investment. Gradually, you will earn some money, and you can always plough it back into your business in order to expand it. Slowly, the business will grow, and within a couple of years, you will realize that you have built some capital.

A young entrepreneur needs to develop a good understanding of the fundamentals of business—never mistake your sales with your profits. If a sale happens, it means part of your capital is coming back into your business; it is *not* a profit you can burn or splurge on. It has to be used to pay your employees, and to repay your loans and your raw material suppliers. It is a trap you have to avoid falling into. During this crucial phase of growth, it is equally essential to ensure that adequate funds are also provided to sustain dependents in your family. Adequate attention needs to be given to their well-being.

LIFE LESSONS

- The transition from being a scientist to a businessman is challenging.
- Don't ever hesitate to chase your dreams.
- Working on your subconscious mind with positive affirmations helps you shape your life.
- Industry associations can act as crucial links between the government and entrepreneurs, facilitating smoother collaboration.
- As an office-bearer of an industry body, engage policymakers to address stakeholders' issues and promote inclusivity.
- Daily entrepreneurial challenges require maturity—and often reveal hidden opportunities for growth and learning.

3
Marketing Mantras

My experience with Jagatjit Industries in Hamira, Punjab, near the India–Pakistan border, was very interesting. I visited the place in the early 1990s, when terrorism in the state had not yet subsided. Normally, when I enter the premises of a corporate office, I go straight to the reception. There, I introduce myself to the receptionists and try to build a rapport. I then find out who holds the authority in the company when it comes to placing orders. The receptionist would invariably tell me the name of the final authority. Once I had this information, I would make a note of it in my records. Next, I would ask about the person responsible for making technical decisions. Once I have gathered all the required details, I will then request an appointment with the person dealing with technical matters.

This is exactly what happened at Jagatjit Industries as well. Once I had secured the appointment, I went and met the technical guy. Once he was convinced, he conducted a small trial and said that the product was 'quite okay'. I then requested him to place an order. He said that he was not authorized to do so, and added that making any modifications to the list of suppliers was the chief executive's prerogative. I then asked him whether I could meet the chief executive. I had already collected the information about the preferences, likes, and dislikes of the top executive. I knew when he was free to meet people, his meal timings, and his busiest hours.

Armed with this information, I went into the chief executive's cabin when I got an appointment. I told him the entire story about the product we manufacture, and that the trial had already been done by his company and that it had worked very well. Then, I asked him to place an order.

He said, 'Okay, I will discuss this with a person and get back to you.'

I said, 'No, Sir, I have come from really far, and Punjab is a hotbed of terrorism. I don't know when or whether I will be able to come again. Kindly place an order right now.'

He said that he was really busy. I then replied, saying that I would wait outside till the time he became free to place the order. He retorted, 'I have told you, go back to Delhi. We will discuss and give you a supply order.'

I said, 'No, Sir, please give me an order right now, so that when I return to my office I can tell my colleagues I have come back with an order.'

He then said, 'Don't waste my time, please go now.'

I refused to budge.

'Do you want me to call the security and throw you out?' asked the chief executive.

I then said, 'Sir, yes, you can throw me out. But throw me out after placing an order.'

Ultimately, the chief executive had to give me an order. Later, the executive and I became good friends. He remarked that he was very impressed with my persuasive powers and my urgency to resolve things then and there. My mantra has always been never to leave things for tomorrow.

▪

There is another episode from the same period of terrorism in Punjab. I was working with a client, Nestlé, in 1990. We had done a lot of technical work in developing the right product for them. Subsequently, I used to visit Moga, which was then one of the nerve centres of terrorism in Punjab. But whenever customers called me, I never missed an opportunity to provide a solution to their problems. On one of these occasions, I received a request to visit the unit in Moga to test our product and resolve a technical issue. As it happened, on the day of my visit, militants demanding a separate homeland for Sikhs (Khalistan) had declared a Punjab bandh, a state-wide shutdown. However, I was not deterred. A few buses were running, as the government was maintaining a skeletal bus service.

I first boarded a bus from Delhi to Ludhiana. From Ludhiana, I could not find any mode of conveyance, as the town lay further within the Punjab heartland, where the bandh was being observed more strictly. Left with few options, I hitched a ride in a police vehicle headed towards Moga. I requested the police to take me along, since I had some urgent work in Moga. Fortunately, the police agreed and came to my assistance. They dropped me inside the factory premises. The government was going the extra mile for those keen on performing their duties despite the bandh called by the extremists.

I entered the factory and realized that it was running and work was on. But they were surprised to see me there. They asked me where I had come from and who had asked me to come on that day. 'We have a prior appointment,' I replied. 'Today is Punjab bandh, and you won't be able to return safely. We can't keep you at the factory,' was their response.

After some discussions, I was asked to return to Delhi immediately. Once again, I took a police van to Ludhiana. From there, I boarded a bus and returned to Delhi at night. That was the kind of commitment that we had to our customers. This is what helped us retain them as well. At Nestlé, they began calling me 'The Sticking Man'. I had developed the reputation of a troubleshooter who could resolve every sticky problem. This helped me strengthen Chemline's relationship with Nestlé and also boost our bottom line.

Whenever Nestlé asked me to develop a product, on the face of it, their demand appeared impossible to fulfil. But invariably, my response would be, 'Okay, we'll do it.' Even though in my heart of hearts, I felt the task was next to impossible, I never said no to the customer. We would get a time period of a week or a month to realize the task. At Nestlé, they acknowledged my never-say-die spirit and often said, 'Dr Goel never said no to us. Even on occasions when the task appeared impossible, he would come close to it and provide us with the solution to our problem.' Nestlé had a reputation for never changing their suppliers, but when I entered the picture, it made an exception to the norm. 'Our relationship with suppliers is permanent, but your case is exceptional. Old suppliers were forgotten and you took their place,' Nestlé officials told me.

Through my approach of providing knowledge to the customers, and with my penchant for never saying no to their demands, I managed to create history! Within two years, in the early 1990s, Chemline captured 80 per cent of India's organized labelling adhesive market. We achieved this feat despite my not being a marketing person. We could achieve this on the basis of sheer transfer of knowledge, discussions, and extending technical help to the customer. In other words, I literally partnered with my clients to find a solution to their challenges.

Getting into the Winning Spirit

Converting challenges into opportunities is something that I have always done. In fact, that is how I lead my life. After proving our mettle with Nestlé, we continued to acquire new clients. It was a fascinating journey of a hands-on approach in selling and developing the market for customized labelling adhesives for breweries, wineries, and distilleries. This was our first big innovation in marketing and product development.

Let me begin with our association with United Breweries Limited (UBL)and United Spirits Limited (USL). Today, these two companies, previously headed by Dr Vijay Mallya, have been taken over by Heineken and Diageo, respectively, but in their heyday, because of them, their parent company, United Breweries, was indeed 'The King of Good Times'. Still, these companies control over 50 per cent of the market in India.[4] I can proudly say that Chemline has been a major supplier (80 per cent) to both of them since we began our association three decades ago.

Our association with UB goes back to 1992. It all began with the technical manager of Mount Shivalik Breweries, Mr R.C. Khanna, getting a job at UB in Bangalore (now Bengaluru). He invited me to a meeting. It was there that he requested me to come up with an adhesive to suit their requirements. 'Our first requirement is that when our beer bottle is dipped in water, the label of the bottle should remain intact. Secondly, the label's adhesive must dissolve when the bottle is placed in hot water, thereby removing the label,' said Mr Khanna.

'Sure, you want it to be cold-water insoluble and hot-water soluble at about 80 degrees. Yes, we can work towards giving you this,' I told him. At that time, most adhesives used to be either casein-based or dextrin-based. Casein is a by-product of milk, and the adhesive was formulated using casein, which was an expensive raw material and wasn't readily available in India; rather, it had to be imported from other countries. I recall that the landed cost of labelling adhesive at the onset of the 1990s was about ₹115 per kg. Moreover, in the alcoholic beverage industry, especially for beer, the adhesive has to work effectively on high-speed labelling machines. These machines operated much faster than those used for ketchup bottles at Nestlé, which we had experience with. They needed a special glue solution, and we successfully managed to develop a synthetic adhesive that met UB's requirements.

At that time, our only competitor in the adhesives industry was a British company that made dextrin-based adhesives. That was a very crude product, which was not suitable for high-speed machines. After a limited shelf life of two to three months, the properties

---

[4]Jainkunia, Nupur, 'Beer vs Spirits: Why UBL Commands Higher Valuation Over USL', *CNBC TV18*, 17 April 2019, https://tinyurl.com/36fkyb5j. Accessed on 7 August 2025.

of the labels would deteriorate. On the other hand, the adhesives we supplied to UB were far more sophisticated and functional. In fact, we discovered that not just UB but the entire beer and spirits industry in India was facing this problem, and it was Chemline that rose to this occasion, offering an economical solution.

How did Chemline achieve the finesse and sophistication to simplify such a complex process? As mentioned, UB's requirement was that the adhesive should be cold-water insoluble and hot-water soluble. The other requirement was that it should have enough stickiness to work on high-speed bottling machines. We researched and began looking for a water-soluble polymer to meet these requirements. My knowledge of polymers and plastics, as well as my demonstrated experience in R&D, came in handy over here. We dissolved a natural polymer into the adhesive to enhance its grip and stickiness. In this way, we came up with an effective yet inexpensive solution for our customers. Gradually, our relationship with the UB Group further strengthened, and all its group companies began using Chemline's adhesive.

After our initial success with the UB Group, Mr S.K. Rastogi, who was then the Technical Manager and in charge of packaging, successfully tested our adhesives and implemented them across all their units nationwide.

Offering such solutions to customers indeed has been a recurring business philosophy for me and Chemline. We work to simplify whatever is complex—whether it is chemistry, business processes, or industry challenges—and come up with the best-possible and most cost-effective solution in the Indian context.

I wish to call this experience 'selling by design and not by chance'. It is far different from the traditional selling of a standard product. Instead, it begins with qualifying the customer's needs and identifying the specific problem for which the prospective customer is trying to find a solution. It is worth spending quality time with the prospective customer on this initial qualifying process, which accounts for almost 60–70 per cent of the time spent in finally selling your product to the customer. The balance time is spent in the final confirmation of the business deal. In the traditional way of selling a standard product, very little time is spent on understanding the customer's needs. If you still manage to get an order by chance, then you may end up handling objections from the customer and face related consequential problems, including delays in the receipt of payment for the products sold. Such experiences taught me that prospective customers like to buy from people they can trust and believe.

The former way of spending quality time creates an emotional bond between the buyer and the seller. In that process of selling, our own self-esteem and self-worth are enhanced, which enables us to discover ourselves and our hidden inner potential, and also derive self-motivation.

▪

At the beginning of my entrepreneurial journey, as I mentioned earlier, I had to wear many hats. At that time, I was an innovator who was coming up with the product idea, developing the process to manufacture the product, and also ensuring the implementation of the idea for production. Apart from this, I was also acting as the marketing representative for Chemline. This included creating awareness about our products in the market and their usefulness to potential clients. In this way, I was involved end-to-end in each of the processes of ideating, producing, and even marketing our products.

Our successful association with Nestlé and UB led to scaling up our ambitions as well as our operations. By 1992, our manpower had increased as well. We had initially put up a 1-tonne reactor at our unit in Kundli. Going forward, we invested in a 5-tonne reactor, along with providing employment to more people.

The manner in which we provided a solution to UB helped build our reputation in the alcoholic beverage industry, which comprises manufacturers of beer, whisky, and wine. Other established names based in North India, such as Mohan Meakin, also started approaching us to supply adhesives for their bottling requirements. Thus, we were getting into the swing of things. With all humility, I can say that when it came to the packaging of beer, wine and whisky, Chemline was being sought after by the biggest names in the industry. I felt like a hero of sorts.

It reached a level when the 'King of Good Times', Dr Vijay Mallya, himself met with me. Along with Dr Mallya, who was the then chairperson, the then President of UB was curious to meet the supplier who was not just good at the science behind the product but also the commercials of the business. Thus, he sought my advice on packaging and labelling their products! I met him at an event where he was meeting all his suppliers in New Delhi, and I had the privilege of getting an award from an industry captain.

I remember going for early morning trials in their Bangalore factory at UB City, where the city's biggest mall of the same name is now located. After a few trials, we had refined and consolidated our product, and I could now afford to travel by air within the country.

I realized that every corner of our country had a distillery. I discovered the extent of the love for whisky in India. It was during the time when UB was becoming a household name at the cost of established names such as Mohan Meakin and Shaw Wallace, which was led by Manu Chhabria. After Mr Chhabria's unfortunate demise while in his fifties, his daughter sold the business, and UB further consolidated its position.

By this time, I had made acquaintance with a wide network of breweries that the UB Group had and travelled across the country, including to breweries in Pondicherry, Kerala, and Maharashtra. Whenever I visited a brewery, distillery, or factory, I used to share life lessons with my customers. I am not an actor, and my face mirrors the emotions that I am going through at that time. I did not restrict myself to my products alone which, at that time, were adhesives but would also discuss the nuances of related products like paper and glass, and shared my thoughts on bottling machines as well. In this way, I went beyond selling my own narrow agenda.

My solution to the customer included complete knowledge of how to apply and remove labels—it was a 360-degree experience. As luck would have it, I got so busy that I never ended up visiting many of these factories again. But whenever my marketing colleagues visited them, even 15–20 years after my visits, the people there would remember me and enquire about me. My colleagues said that the people there had been excited to interact with me during that single visit. They remembered the 360-degree knowledge that I had imparted about the entire journey of an adhesive, including knowledge of paper, printing, glass, and inks.

All of this happened because I had stuck to my mantra of marketing—namely, selling by design and not by chance. That is what I tell my colleagues in marketing. Whenever you visit a customer as a supplier, display complete transparency. That's something they will appreciate. Go with commitment and knowledge. Enrich the customer with a lot of knowledge. Once you do that, they will always remember you.

Let me share an interesting incident here. Satnam Singh, a manufacturer who had started manufacturing labelling machines in India, called me one day. He said that he needed an adhesive from us and added, 'Whichever distillery we go to, they say our machine must work on Chemline's adhesive. You are the only manufacturer of the adhesive they love.' Because of the commitment I displayed in helping customers find a solution, every distillery was familiar with our product.

I employed an innovative marketing device to ensure that our product stood out to distilleries. I would use a plastic pouch that contained around 10 gm of our transparent adhesive, and then sealed the pouch and stapled it with the mail letter. (In those days, all marketing efforts were dependent on the postal mode and direct mailers.) I would then send the pouch, the size of a shampoo sachet, in the envelope, along with our marketing communications. That transparent and gooey sachet stood out and became a hit with the distillery staff. It was the best and most economical advertising I could hope to get for Chemline. It was a tribute to the quality and visibility of our adhesive.

A time came when our brand found mention as the adhesive supplier in the project reports of distilleries and breweries, even before the project took off, at the blueprint stage itself. If it was good enough for Kingfisher, it was good enough for every other Indian brand at that time! That's the kind of success we achieved in our formative years in the early 1990s.

Much before 1993, I had repaid all my creditors, along with the interest that had accrued after the closure of Macro Vinyls and during the period of setting up and consolidating Chemline. In 1993, my sister got married. At this point, my father requested me to pitch in towards the expenses for the wedding. By the grace of God, I had attained enough financial stability by then. I decided to bear most of the expenses for the wedding, and we hosted a grand ceremony in a banquet hall. More than anybody else, it was my relatives in the extended family who appeared to be pleasantly surprised. They appreciated how I had bounced back from the multiple setbacks I had faced and stepped forward to pitch in for this important family event at a prestigious venue. I was simply going by the guiding principle and life credo—the more you give, the more you get back.

Another guiding principle I discovered is that when you miss something great and beautiful, you create something to fill that vacuum that is just as beautiful or even greater. You go into a creative mode to fill that gap. To overcome the feeling of loss, I worked hard, sometimes even 14 hours a day. I began to create something to become relevant in this world. This beauty of creation had just begun!

On this note, let me recount an example that demonstrates the manner in which we dominated the market of labelling adhesives between 1992 and 1994. A British company, Corn Products of India, that is no longer in operation, was one that produced starch from corn and subsequently made glue from it. Chemline's entry into the market hit them hard. Their product sales were plummeting. Within two years, their sales approached zero. I even received a letter from them. They said, 'You have taken a total share of our business. You are a company that can buy us out.' Of course, I was not in a position to take over a British company.

Our rise in the sector can be a case study in product development and marketing management. It can illustrate how a company can reverse the existing market situations within two years. I was a non-marketing founder-entrepreneur to begin with. When I ventured into the field of marketing, my colleagues told me that it wasn't 'my cup of tea' and that, at the most, I could be a technical person. I proved all the naysayers wrong by capturing 80 per cent of the organized market for labelling adhesives for India's beer and spirits industry.

Chemline was fortunate that our first few clients were in the organized sector. Nestlé had four to five factories, UB had around 30 factories, and USL had another 50 factories. Mohan Meakin had about seven factories and Shaw Wallace had more than 20 factories. Once you got your product approved at one of these, the others followed suit, and it was implemented in all the production units. In the organized sector, one had to market the product in one place, and it would get replicated in 10 other places. The crux of our marketing initiatives in the B2B (business-to-business) segment was imparting knowledge to our customers and providing solutions to their most intricate problems.

Ideas of Innovations

What was the next step for Chemline in the food and spirits packaging industries, after having experienced success with Nestlé, UB, and USL?

In the wave of our success with the adhesives for the food

and spirits packaging industry, I happened to visit Düsseldorf in Germany in the year 2000 for a trade exhibition called Drupa. Chemline was one of the participants from India at this exhibition, along with major international players in the printing and packaging segment. I surveyed the products that were being used around the globe and the futuristic cutting-edge technologies being displayed by the participants. It was here that I got the idea for my next innovation!

I saw a Billhöfer (a German company) machine that was using an adhesive for laminating film onto a printing board. Normally, all the cartons—be it the mono cartons used for Nestlé's baby cereals, or boxes for medicines, tissue papers, and the like—have film laminated on them. After the printing, the film lamination serves as a protective layer on the printed board. It also adds gloss to the print and makes the box sturdy. At the exhibition, I saw that film lamination was being done on a fully automatic high-speed lamination machine.

At that time, those kinds of machines had started coming into India, but there was no suitable adhesive available for them in our country. One or two Indian companies were importing the requisite dry lamination adhesive from Taiwan, but it was a very expensive proposition. I keenly observed the performance of the machine with that adhesive. I discreetly procured a sample from the exhibition and brought it back with me to India. I then worked on it further over the next year.

Let me now explain why the manufacture of dry lamination adhesive by Chemline was such a breakthrough in the Indian market in the early 2000s. Earlier, manual lamination machines were used in the industry, which was a much slower process. Running at 60 m a minute for the lamination process, the new machines were at least 10 times faster than manual machines and enhanced productivity with better quality and efficiency.

Curiously, neither world market leaders—Henkel or Pidilite—who were doing business in India manufactured dry lamination adhesive at that time. So, Chemline has the distinction of being the first company to begin manufacturing dry lamination adhesive in India. With this, we acquired the first-mover advantage. At that time, the top Indian companies that manufactured packaging for FMCG (fast-moving consumer goods) companies—such as

Unilever, Nestlé, and other food and pharmaceutical companies in India—were all on the lookout for such an adhesive. When we approached the packaging companies with our product and offered it for testing, they were very happy with the quality. Our laminating adhesive began flying off the shelves. Over the next few months, we also made further improvements to the product on the basis of industry feedback.

Having consolidated our market share at home, we set our sights higher. We began exporting our adhesive to prospective customers in Europe, Latin America and West Asia. Today, I am proud to share that we are exporting to industrially advanced countries such as Germany. In a way, it has come full circle. Having found the initial inspiration from a trade exhibition in Germany, now we are in a position where our technical know-how and product knowledge can rival—or even better—the best in the world. This success made Chemline a leader in the supply of adhesives for the printing and packaging industry in the early 2000s. Chemline's scale and range of operations were expanding and, as discussed earlier, we set up a new plant in Dhaturi, near Murthal, on a piece of land that was 10 times the size of our first unit at Kundli.

Along with staple products such as transparent tape, we began manufacturing novel products such as dry lamination adhesive from the premises of our new factory. The first big name to order this novel product was Bharat Box Factory, one of the leaders in the mono-carton space in the 2000s. Twentieth Century Packaging Limited was our next big client for dry lamination adhesive. The printing industry in the country was much larger than the alcoholic beverage industry that we had initially ventured into. The scale of our operations and our sales turnover benefited immensely from our new foray into this industry segment.

With our innovation and first-mover advantage, Chemline became a comprehensive supplier catering to the requirements of the printing and packaging industry in India. Along with this, we began providing a bouquet of allied products and services to the industry as well. Chemline started gaining popularity and became a name to reckon with in the printing and packaging industry in India.

LIFE LESSONS

- My mantra has always been never to leave things for tomorrow—settle the matter then and there.
- Never turn down your customers' requests or concerns.
- Always make an effort to share knowledge with your customers.
- Provide solutions to clients' problems, wherever possible.
- Stay honest and transparent with your clients and never mislead them.
- Simplifying things—whether manufacturing processes or formulations for product development—is the best way to succeed.
- Transparency and trust are the surest way to win customers.
- Work in partnership with your customer for value addition.
- Constant innovation keeps you at the forefront of the marketplace.
- Let good thoughts come from all directions and embrace them.
- Adapt the best global practices that set benchmarks of excellence.

PART II

Life Sutras

4

Life Sutras for Growth and Healthy Living

Over the years, as I did various experiments in the laboratory of life, I discovered a few principles for growth and healthy living. In this chapter, I intend to share these uplifting lessons that have worked as guiding lights for me. I have developed these sets of principles during the process of setting up Chemline and navigating the challenges and opportunities that it brought along with it.

Listen to Your Inner Voice

Have you ever listened to your inner voice to visualize your future? Have you connected with your inner guiding system, delving deeply into the process?

Right from the beginning, I developed the habit of writing in my diary before going to sleep. During this process, I would engage in deep thinking and contemplation (*chintan*) on the day's happenings, along with my observations and feelings about life. *Chintan ke in anubhavon ko main diary main likhta tha*—I would capture these profound experiences of reflection and contemplation in the pages of my diary.

At many times, these experiences would turn into poetry or into visualizations about the future. I discovered that such processes and daily habits had helped me be in touch with my inner being, and that, in turn, gave me inspiration, showed me a path, and provided solutions to my day-to-day challenges.

During one of these exercises of chintan, I visualized that I'm destined to evolve and progress and become a well-known industrialist one day. At that time, I was without a job and surrounded by a number of life challenges. I started doing this process of chintan and visualization during pranayama and meditation as well. I have always felt that during such meditation processes, I rise above mundane thoughts and concerns. I would reach a state of consciousness in which I was able to forgive and support even those individuals who had been critical of me. Later, I termed this process as 'getting in touch with yourself'.

When I began looking inward for answers, I grappled with a lot of questions and problems, including anxiety and depression. Then, as mentioned earlier, one fine December evening, I wrote down in my diary that my destination was different and that I would not let the circumstances bog me down. I visualized a future for myself as an established and globally well-known entrepreneur and industrialist. Listening to my inner voice gave me direction and vision for the future. I started working on the vision that was thus created.

One has to develop this trait; that is the first step. Listen to this divine voice inside you that gives you a direction for life. It is only possible to find this voice when you look within, and not by going out, talking to people, or reading books. This is a great source of wisdom!

To develop this habit, you need to sit in a quiet corner early in the morning or late at night. Close your eyes and breathe deeply (preferably do pranayama). Slowly, you will reach a state of quieting of your mind. Your inner voice will start becoming clearer, and then you can speak with yourself and visualize the way forward. You must review your life on a regular basis and do meditation. When you reach the meditative state, you reach a point where the quality of your thoughts far outweighs the quantity of thoughts—the number of thoughts coming to your mind goes down and the quality goes up. When this happens, it will show you the ways to emerge victorious from the present-day challenges affecting you and will help you visualize a brighter future.

What can you do to make your inner voice stronger? As far as I understand, working with honesty and transparency makes your personality stronger. When you work with honesty, your inner confidence goes up. On the other hand, if you indulge in wrongdoings, the intensity of your inner voice tends to become feeble. The weaker your inner voice becomes, the easier it is to keep ignoring it. It is important to recognize this pattern and put a stop to it.

If you have a level of trust with an associate, they won't hesitate to work with you. Even if a person is not the most intelligent one around, their trustworthiness can help propel them forward in life. This, too, helps you strengthen your inner voice. When you talk to yourself, a hazy image of what needs to be done in the present (as well as in the future) will dance before your eyes. This will help you develop a vision.

It is when I visualized that I would be a successful entrepreneur and globally recognized industrialist one day that I began working towards achieving that goal. But the first step is developing that vision, and the next requisite is possessing the traits of honesty, trustworthiness, and forgiveness. With the possession of these traits, you will be able to successfully overcome the challenges you encounter while moving towards your goal.

Arm Yourself with Character

When you have found your inner voice and imagined the direction your life must take, you must be equipped with a good personality and character. If you don't possess these personality traits and character to begin with, you will struggle to even visualize your future, as your inner voice may not be strong enough.

Now, let's elaborate upon life values and character. Taking

shortcuts and being dishonest will not serve you in the long run if you are starting your business or, for that matter, taking any new initiative in life. I have always believed that the greatest values of life include being honest, trustworthy, and forgiving. We have to practise this in our day-to-day life.

Even if you have already embarked on your journey, in order to navigate the path ahead and overcome the obstacles on the way, you will require good teammates and associates. These team members, business associates, or partners will only join your journey provided you have these character traits. Only with these traits will you be able to take the right people along and convince them to join your cause and work towards a common mission. That is why having a good character and personality, and leading by example, are so important.

Over the years, my esteemed colleagues and associates have joined me in the Chemline journey because they realized that I was one of them—working hard and leading by example. They believed that I was a business leader who could be trusted. They felt that I was an honest leader and that their careers were safe at Chemline. That is why sincerity of purpose and trustworthiness are crucial character traits for any leader.

Several times in my career, I have asked people why they have bestowed their trust in me and wished to join us at Chemline. More often than not, the answers were very similar: they believed that the leader at Chemline was a straightforward person who was honest in his dealings. Most recently, one of Haryana's leading academicians indicated a similar desire. When I asked him why he was interested, he said: 'You are a truthful, simple person, without malice or any hidden agenda. That is why I want to be associated with you. In hindsight, I think I should have joined your business mission 15 years ago.'

Another aspect related to this is how you carry yourself—your personality traits are manifested on your face and in the manner in which you converse with others. Let's say I go to meet a prospective partner, client, or business associate. Within the first few minutes of our interaction, they will be able to assess and read my character. My experience over my more-than-three-decade-long corporate journey has been this—whether it is a customer, business associate, or a government official, within a few minutes of meeting me, people make up their mind to associate with me and my company.

Always Move Forward, Never Take a Step Back

A good way to approach your goals is by breaking down a big goal into smaller goals and making small contributions on a day-to-day basis. Even if you make only a small progress every day, you must ensure not to retreat. The idea is to consistently keep moving forward. I believe every individual can transform their lives by following this golden principle.

On that note, I would like to share my experience of trekking to the Amarnath Cave at the age of 65, with no prior experience of mountain trekking. We set out with a group of friends on the 46-km trek from Pahalgam to the Amarnath Cave, situated at a height of 12,760 feet above sea level. The route was very rough, with rain and snow along the way making progress even more difficult. Despite these hurdles, we continued moving steadily towards the cave. On the last stretch, we were exhausted, but we did not give up. Finally, we reached closer and could see the cave from a distance.

The sight of the cave gave us further strength to keep moving. At last, we reached our destination—climbing the stairs to have the darshan of the *shivling*. At that time, I had tears in my eyes. Looking back at the tough journey, it felt almost unbelievable. This could be made possible only because we kept moving forward despite all difficulties. We paused along the way to relax, gathered strength, and moved on. This journey remains one of the greatest lessons of my life: always move forward and never take a step back!

Monitoring Your Thinking Process

Your present thoughts often decide how you want to lead your life. Your life today is a sum total of your thoughts.

Your mind may be filled with all kinds of thoughts. If you channel them in a creative, positive, and purposeful direction, you can achieve bigger and better things in life. One must train the mind to engage in purposeful, beautiful, and creative thoughts. Therefore, it is important that we look at what our thinking process must entail and monitor it closely.

Thus, looking back is just as important as looking forward.

Our thinking process indirectly shapes our lives, as celebrated author Rhonda Byrne notes in her iconic book *The Secret*. She writes that we become what we think. The thoughts in our mind can be of various kinds: creative, positive, and powerful, or wasteful and negative. Once you observe your thinking process minutely, you will be able to filter out the negative and retain the powerful, positive, and creative. In my view, one must try to remain in a state wherein you have maximum creative and purposeful thoughts. It isn't always easy; when you are gripped with anxiety or surrounded by difficulties, the mind tends to drift into negativity.

You can blame your circumstances or hold other people or the Almighty responsible for the problems you are grappling with, or you can accept the situation you are in and view these problems as ultimately being beneficial for you. As A.P.J. Abdul Kalam, the people's president, has observed in his inspirational book *Wings of Fire*, 'Why be afraid of difficulties, sufferings, and problems? When troubles come, try to understand the relevance of your sufferings. Adversity always presents opportunities for introspection. [...] When your hopes and dreams and goals are dashed, search among the wreckage, you may find a golden opportunity hidden in the ruins.'[5]

---

[5]Kalam, A.P.J. Abdul, and Arun Tiwari, *Wings of Fire*, Universities Press, Hyderabad, 1999, 5 and 140.

Maintain a state where you keep your thinking positive, creative, and purposeful. Divide your day in such a manner that most of your time is engaged in purposeful activities. Don't think about harming anybody or being negative about others. If you think positively, you are creating a positive world around you, full of possibilities.

Whatever we think is sent out as vibes to the world. So, avoid sending out negative vibes. Once you are determined and resolute in your thinking, you can achieve even those goals that looked impossible when you first thought of them. Therefore, my advice to the younger generation is: 'Keep your thoughts elevated. Take control of your thinking process for healthy living and go on to achieve greater heights.'

If your thinking process is focused on trivial matters, you cannot hope to achieve big goals. On the other hand, if your thinking process is deep, positive, and purposeful, it will lead to you achieving bigger goals in life. It will also equip you with the self-esteem and confidence to be a useful member of society.

When You Give, You Receive in Multiples

The more you give, the more you get back—this applies to every sphere of life. If you send out negativity, you will get it back in good measure. If you send out positive vibes, you will receive them in multiples.

When I launched Chemline and thought of manufacturing labelling adhesives, I experienced this principle firsthand. I was vindicated about this belief at several other points in my life as well. At the onset of my business journey, when a former associate needed adhesives for use on acrylic sheets, I was generous in imparting wisdom and helping him out. The activity was never transactional and was, in essence, selfless. I believe this selflessness was repaid in good measure to me throughout the Chemline journey.

'You are the creator of knowledge, ideas and wisdom. To gain new ideas, share your ideas. Unless you give, you do not create.'

This is my firm conviction. Normally, teachers and professors are creators of knowledge. The wisdom they share with their students benefits society. They create something of value by sharing their knowledge, and in this manner multiply their wisdom and knowledge as well. When you let these principles guide you in your life, you will automatically become more creative and make things that are useful for society. When you do that, people will appreciate you.

If everybody begins following this principle, a critical mass can be achieved. There will be so much positivity created that it will be extremely beneficial for all of society. Those who contribute to others will also benefit in a mutual manner. Whether it is love, happiness, wisdom, or knowledge, you receive it back in multiples. That is my abiding belief and guiding principle!

As a number of ancient philosophers and saints have said, 'You are here to give, not to take.' You are here to render service to mankind. When you render service, you derive happiness and satisfaction.

Staying in a Happy State of Mind

Now, let us dwell a little on the concept of happiness. How can you stay in a blissful, happy state of mind?

To begin with, keep a smiling face as much as you can. When you meet a new acquaintance, greet them with a smile. It will take away the stress and tension from everyone you meet, as well as yourself. Life itself is interesting; learn to smile at life. If you can't make it, just fake it. I believe that if I am undergoing a challenging phase in my life, and I smile at the situation, I will come out of it unscathed. Otherwise, I may slide into depression. These are a few things that one needs to put into practice.

It is a well-known fact that your creative faculties multiply when you are in a happy state of mind. If you are sad, your creative faculties will stall. So, if you want to multiply your creative faculties, you need to be in a happy state of mind. You must be happy with your life, surroundings, and situations. You must excitedly appreciate them. When you feel happy from within, you will exude positivity.

Positive thinking, positive voice, and positive words—always use these. This is the biggest principle of management: when you have to work with other people. Even if somebody makes a mistake, say positive things. Tell them that they used to do so well, and encourage them to become a little better. You must identify the potential and power within. That's how your colleague will feel motivated and search hard for their hidden potential and talent.

By remaining happy, we nurture our body and mind, and stay healthy. Taking care of oneself is one's primary responsibility towards oneself. If you stay happy, your health will be good. So, stay happy and nurture your soul.

Converting Challenges into Opportunities

This has been the central theme of my life. Let me explain this to you with an example. Challenges are like an opportunity for me to explore myself. Currently, amid ongoing challenges both in professional work and personal life, I have made great strides in business as well as personal well-being, even leading to a new phase of my life. I have expanded my business, I am writing my memoir, I am putting together a book of my poems, I am learning music and photography, and I have revived my childhood passion for painting. I recently visited the picturesque mountains of Uttarakhand and saw nature in its pristine form in the Himalayas. I have been able to carve out time to explore and discover a new phase of life these days. I have used all these activities as opportunities for self-growth and self-control.

Every adverse situation has some opportunity hidden within it. Testing times and trials by fire help you emerge stronger. When you face challenges in life, you can exercise two options. One, to give in to pain, become stressed and unhappy, or to embrace them as opportunities. When you see challenges in this way, your

willpower increases, your energy grows manifold, and you discover within yourself the ability to overcome any crisis.

Perceive a challenge as a transformational state that needs to be overcome as quickly as possible. These are things you will overcome and remember for a long time. The first time I faced family challenges and subsequent parting, I was in a state of shock, sorrow and depression. But I overcame it all to bounce back and proactively launch a company from scratch. I harnessed the gains I made during a testing period into opportunities. Today, those times are sweet memories for me. Similarly, I want to convert the present phase of life into a sweet memory as well.

I welcome tough situations. I feel that somebody who has had an easy life can never attain maturity. So, at times, I tell my people to come out of their comfort zone on their own. Ask yourself, 'What have I got used to?' If you want to learn from life, leave your comfort zone behind and embrace tougher situations. Our Prime Minister, Narendra Modi, is an epitome of this philosophy. During the pandemic, when China trespassed into the country, everybody saw it as a national crisis. But ultimately, India emerged stronger from it. We didn't get intimidated by Beijing and pushed back for the first time since the defeat in the 1962 war. What looked like a difficult situation made India emerge as a stronger country. Today, China will think twice before making any such audacious attempt. It was a tough situation, but Prime Minister Modi converted it into an opportunity for the country. This is a classic example of how one must welcome tough situations!

Every moment of life needs to be celebrated and enjoyed. For instance, the late philosopher Osho said that one must even celebrate death. I believe that when you celebrate every moment and situation of life as it emerges, you can evolve into a much better human being. I have no regrets at this stage in life. I look at the big picture and view every challenge as an opportunity. These challenges are a phase of life that is full of learning and needs to be enjoyed.

The Power of Affirmation

One of my esteemed colleagues at Chemline recently mentioned that what she enjoys most during our yoga and meditation sessions is the affirmations I lead at the end. I could not agree more with

her. This part of our interaction is always both interesting and inspiring. For example, during one of the affirmations, I say, 'I am happy and I am healthy. I keep my body and mind fit by doing yoga, meditation, and pranayama every day. I also keep my mind creative and positive through the regular practice of meditation and pranayama. I enjoy every moment of my life and share that joy with others as well.' I also remind my colleagues that whatever you share with others comes back to you in multiples. Not just this, I also affirm: 'I will adapt myself to every circumstance and enjoy myself in every circumstance'.

At the end of the affirmations, we pray for the good health and well-being of all living beings. Our thoughts directly manifest in our lives, for life is the summation of our thinking process.

The Power of Appreciation

Appreciate yourself, appreciate co-workers, family members, and people in society. Welcome circumstances as they come to you and thank God for whatever is given to you.

Appreciation brings happiness, motivation, and positivity, and boosts confidence in the person being appreciated as well as in the appreciator. It brings in positive circumstances and situations which lead to overall growth.

Here are some quotes that I found during my reading that share this ideal:

'The roots of all goodness lie in the soil of appreciation for goodness.'
—Dalai Lama

'As we express our gratitude, we must never forget that the highest appreciation is not to utter words but to live by them.'
—John F. Kennedy

'I would maintain that thanks are the highest form of thought; and that gratitude is happiness doubled by wonder.'
—G.K. Chesterton

'Feeling gratitude and not expressing it is like wrapping a present and not giving it.'
—William Arthur Ward

'Trade your expectations for appreciation and your whole world changes instantly.'
—Tony Robbins

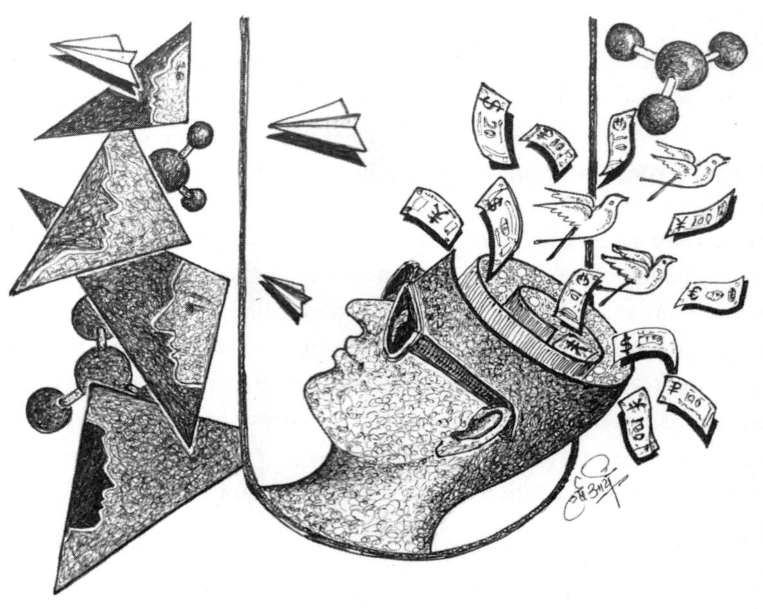

Harness the Power of Human Capital

I was recently discussing matters related to human capital development, particularly our manpower requirement, with the CEO of Chemline.

Let's say that, after this financial year, the turnover is X million (or 1.25 X million or 1.5 X million). We would look at the profit before tax in each case, and accordingly, look at the remaining profit and the investment to be made in recruiting new people. Sometimes, we are not able to assess the money that must be kept aside to acquire new talent.

A new entrepreneur will be very hesitant to spend large amounts of money on salaries. Till very recently, I was among the entrepreneurs who were hesitant about spending large amounts of money on human capital. Over my journey of 35 years, I was hesitant to pay really high salaries. But now, I can see the benefits of doing so. My CEO and I have already begun discussions regarding our human capital requirements. To grow, a new company must invest in getting the right kind of human resources. The right kind of human resource may need more money, but new entrepreneurs are not always prepared to pay this.

To do away with these reservations, you need to work backwards and look at the commensurate increase in sales. This can help you decide whether it is worthwhile to invest in getting a professional with a high salary or not. When we did this, we were surprised to discover that we could afford to set aside a significant amount to acquire new talent. Now, we have realized that we can assign a larger allocation for new human resources. We have set up several new projects, but many of these need to be manned properly. For that, we can immediately allocate a sizeable amount for our manpower requirements. This will enhance the efficiency and subsequently, the output of new projects.

Until now, I had not been able to comprehend the true value of investing in human capital. Consulting our HR department, along with the CEO, has helped me arrive at the vision of investing larger amounts in human capital. There is a saying in Hindi, *Sasta roye baar baar, mehanga roye ek baar*, which translates to: 'What is cheap makes you cry several times, but what is expensive will make you cry just once'. This aptly encapsulates the sentiment expressed above.

Large companies or conglomerates spend lakhs on head-hunting firms just to locate the right talent, suitable for specific assignments. The mantra is to get the right person for the right job. Once the right person is in place, they must also get the freedom to execute business plans. Along with the freedom comes the responsibility of meeting the deliverables.

I have reached a stage where I wish to delegate some of my hands-on responsibilities for running the organization to the CEO.

By doing this, I can focus on strategies for expanding Chemline into new verticals. My expertise in creating new ventures can help the company achieve greater, exponential returns by making forays into fresh segments and business lines.

As it is, for a small company, we already have 10 different verticals. We are into labelling adhesives, printing and packaging adhesives, speciality hot-melt adhesives, printed labels, label stocks, rigid packaging, metallized papers, coated papers, printing inks and coatings, and industrial tapes. Going forward, I have visualized that each vertical of Chemline can become a company in itself if we pay adequate attention to our human resources. We can look at appointing a leader for each vertical, who can lead it to much larger growth than what we have achieved in all these years. All this would be done under the flagship of Chemline.

I have noticed another perceptible trend in human resource development. In the beginning, we simply could not afford to have non-performers. However, during the recruitment process, at times, you can end up with a few. Naturally, a young entrepreneur would not tolerate this and might be inclined to dismiss such employees outright. Yet, within the dynamics of the Indian workplace, this isn't always an easy option. Removing one non-performer can create an atmosphere of uncertainty, causing even those performing well to feel threatened and insecure. You may try to explain to them that their jobs are safe, that the dismissal has been done to make the company leaner and more efficient, but such explanations are futile at times. As the Hindi saying goes, *Ek chidiya ke udne se saari chidiya ud jaati hain*—'If one bird flies away, the entire flock may take flight'—aptly encapsulating this predicament.

That is how employee psychology tends to work most of the time. While retaining the best talent is crucial for the organization, it is equally important to reassure less efficient workers that their jobs are not at risk. In this way, we are able to harness the capabilities of the laggards as well. The message that goes out to the workforce is this: 'Here is the top management of a stable organization. Even if tomorrow we make a mistake, our jobs will be safe.' This serves as a big morale booster for the workers and, ultimately, results in higher profits and greater revenue for the organization.

If you back your people, in the long run, they will provide results. This is the strategy of harnessing your human capital with a touch of compassion. It is a departure from the West, especially the US, in which many organizations believe in the concept of hire and fire. This policy of hire and fire cannot work in the Indian context! I have observed that seasoned employees, who have been working for a long time with Chemline, display a high degree of loyalty. One develops a comfort level working with such employees. They treat their organization like their own family. That is the level of trust that we want to achieve.

We believe in providing hands-on training to our employees and offering them mentorship. Based on the current profitability of the company, we have realized that we can afford to invest in expanding our human resources. The only requisite is that the resource that is hired must bring in revenue and sales to the organization.

Moreover, we have adopted the concept of fixed and variable components in the employee's salary to reward performance. We have enhanced the variable component by as much as 50 per cent for those employees who want to avail of performance-linked incentives. I understand that in Europe, variable salaries make up to about 60 to 70 per cent of a person's cost to the company. In India, variable salaries are lower in comparison. So, by deciding to implement variable salaries, we are inspiring our employees to work harder. In this way, we have nurtured a culture of meritocracy at Chemline.

In the market, our employees have developed a reputation for being solutions providers. Therefore, they are really sought-after by our competitors. We are like an institute and a great training ground. Of late, we have decided to attempt to retain our best talent rather than allowing them to get poached by a rival company. We do this even if it means matching the salary packages, or even exceeding them. We would prefer to pay them a little extra rather than seeing them join another company and become our competitors. We would want to retain the talent in our company, no matter what it takes.

The real test of a good employer comes during challenging times. For instance, during the Covid-19 pandemic, we did not retrench any staff. Rather, we went the extra mile to make them feel comfortable. We extended the work-from-home facility to our employees, and full salaries were paid for the entire duration of the lockdown necessitated by the pandemic. Even now, we remain very liberal with flexi-time and work-from-home arrangements. Even when we were compelled to make some wage cuts at the peak of the pandemic, we reimbursed all affected employees once the situation had normalized.

Most good workplaces remunerate their employees fairly, provide them with good facilities and, more importantly, treat them well. But treating them well is just the beginning—we must ensure that we treat them as equals. An egalitarian work culture, where the chief executive and shop-floor worker eat in the same place, is something I observed in Western countries and later implemented at Chemline. That is where a lack of hierarchy, which is part of an organizational culture that I have developed at Chemline, can play a big part in developing loyalty towards the organization as well as the management. Indeed, I have ensured that Chemline has evolved into a hierarchy-free organization with a flat structure, where anyone can approach me directly. For those who look from the outside, this lack of hierarchy may appear unusual, but for me, there have never been silos that distance me from my workers, managers, or colleagues. I have never harboured such distinctions throughout my career.

The CEO and the employee must merge their identities. The CEO must function as if he were any other employee. On the other hand, the employee must display ownership of the company as if he were the CEO. This is the mantra for creating organizations and ensuring that they continue to flourish.

Time and Transformation

Change is a constant in life. The situations and people around us never remain static. Transformation is the law of nature; everything changes with time. Therefore, we must evolve at the same pace and adapt to new situations. Those who do not change will eventually perish. In relation to this transformation, the person who continually adapts to change reaches new heights in life and achieves success. I have explained this theme through several of my poems dedicated to change and transformation.

The first poem focuses on time, which is intrinsically linked to transformation.

परिवर्तन ही जीवन है

मेरे बंधू, मेरे मीत,
जब यूँ होता था,
तब सब ठीक लगता था,
क्योंकि, हमेशा यूँ ही होता आया,
परंतु जब इसमें परिवर्तन आया,
तो हम समझ न पाए,
बस एक एहसास था.कि ये ठीक न हुआ|
परंतु मेरे बंधु, मेरे मीत
हमें बदलना है खुद को, बदलना है नजरिये को,
बदलना है मन को|
क्योंकि,
जब यूँ होता था तब भी ठीक था,
अब ऐसा हुआ तब भी ठीक है|
ऐसे में मत घबराना तुम,
क्योंकि,
घटनाएं तो बदलती रहेंगी,
घटनाओं का बदलना ही जीवन है|
तो बदल लो खुद को घटनाओं के साथ||

Change Is the Essence of Life

My friend, my brother,
When it happened a certain way,
Everything felt good,
For it had always been happening that way.
But when it changed,
We couldn't understand what was happening—
Only the realization that what had happened
was not something good.

But, my friend, my brother,

We need to change ourselves,
Change our points of view,
And change the desires of our hearts.
For when it happened that way, it was fine,
And when it is happening this way, it is also fine.
You must not get daunted by new circumstances,
For circumstances will keep changing.
The change of circumstances is the very essence of life,
So change yourself along with the circumstances.
The sentiments also find resonance in that evergreen song,
sung by Mohammed Rafi,
from the Dev Anand starrer *Hum Dono*:

मैं ज़िन्दगी का साथ निभाता चला गया
हर फ़िक्र को धुएँ में उड़ाता चला गया|
बर्बादियों का सोग मनाना फ़ुज़ूल था,
बरबादियों का जश्न मनाता चला गया||

I kept going with whatever life brought to me.
I let every worry drift away in a whiff of smoke.
It was useless to mourn over the disasters in my life,
So I kept on celebrating these disasters.
This, in essence, is the crux—and, in a way, the
philosophy—of my life.
Here is another poem in a similar vein.

इन वर्षों ने मुझे कितना बदल दिया

इन वर्षों ने मुझे कितना बदल दिया
मैं कैसा था, मैं कैसा बन गया?
इन वर्षों ने मुझे कितना बदल दिया|

इन वर्षों की यात्राएं,
इन वर्षों के यह अनुभव,
मैं क्या से क्या हो गया?
मैं वैसा नहीं रहा जैसा पहले था|

इतना बदलने के पश्चात्
मुझे और बदलते रहना है,
मुझे परिवर्तित होते रहना है,
परिवर्तित होते रहना है|

परिवर्तन रुकेगा नहीं
आगे आने वाले वर्ष
मुझे कितना और बदलेंगे ?
मेरी यह परिवर्तित होती जिंदगी,
तेज़ रफ़्तार से परिवर्तित होती जिंदगी,
कहाँ जाकर रुकेगी?
कुछ पता नहीं,
कुछ पता नहीं!

How Much Have These Years Transformed Me

How much have these years transformed me
What was I before? And what have I become?
How much have these years transformed me

The journeys and experiences of these years
Have changed me dramatically
I am not what I once was.
Still, despite changing so much,
I must continue to change even more,
I must keep transforming,
I must keep transforming.

The change will not stop here.
How much will the years to come transform me?
When and where will this transformation—
Which is happening at such a quick pace—come to an end
I don't know anything about this yet.

The rainy season of August is very humid, and the sultry heat gradually recedes during this time. As the season progresses, humidity lessens, and the mornings and evenings become pleasant.

This change in the weather brings with it a sense that time has moved on—the rains have ended, and the pleasant, cool air has replaced the damp humidity. This, in turn, gives me a feeling of change and transformation, which prompted me to write this piece of poetry.

आगे बढ़ते जाना

समय तेज़ गति से आगे बढ़ता,
हम रह गए पीछे ऐसा लगता|
हमें भी बढ़ना है आगे समय के साथ
जैसे सितम्बर के आने से वर्षा ऋतु होती है समाप्त
उमस कम होने लगती
भोर–साँझ सुहावना मौसम
जो देता समय के आगे बढ़ने का एहसास |

ध्यान रखना मेरे मीत!
पीछे न रह जाना तुम भी
जो कुछ छूट गया, रह गया करने से
उसे न जाना भूल|
समय के साथ
आगे बढ़ते जाना
आगे बढ़ते जाना||

Keep Moving Forward

Time moves forward at lightning speed;
I feel as though I have been left behind.
Yet I, too, must move forward with time.
Just as the arrival of September
Announces the end of the rainy season,
The humidity fades away,
The weather is lovely in the mornings and evenings,
Reminding us of the change in time.

Remember this, my brother and friend:
Do not allow yourself to be left behind.

Do not forget what still remains to be done.
Keep moving forward,
Keep moving forward,
In step with time.

The next poem also relates to moving on in life.

LIFE LESSONS

- The reward of honesty is a stronger inner voice.
- The more you share, the more you create.
- Our greatest asset in life is good health. Taking care of it is our prime responsibility.
- Develop the habit of reading and learning for educational and mental growth.
- Pranayama, dhyān, and maun improve mental health.
- Reflecting on who you are is a crucial exercise.
- Appreciate yourself, your co-workers, your family members, and other people in society.
- Retain talent in your organization at all costs.
- Motivate and train underperformers to improve efficiency, as the West's 'hire and fire' policies do not work in India.
- Be willing to pay well to attract the best talent in the industry.
- Treat employees as equals and foster an egalitarian, non-discriminatory work culture.
- Change is the only constant in life—so remain mentally flexible and keep adapting.

5

Importance of Spiritual Practices

Spiritual practices offer an anchor in life's turbulent seas, nurturing inner peace, clarity, and resilience. They connect us to something greater than ourselves, guiding our thoughts, actions, and purpose.

The Power of Meditation and Yoga

Yoga and meditation helped me overcome the seemingly insurmountable challenges in my life and convert them into opportunities. At a very young age, my father initiated me, as well as some of our other family members, into yoga and took us to Dhirendra Brahmachari's Vishwayatan Yogashram in New Delhi. The process that began then was carried forward by learning from other masters such as Sri Sri Ravi Shankar and Baba Ramdev.

Having experienced the importance of yoga and meditation in my own life, I thought I must share my experience and knowledge of the two with every member of my company. With this objective, I introduced yoga lessons in our company in the year 2019. We began with a yoga class every day, and a mandatory yoga class on Saturdays and Sundays. Every day, we start our yoga class at 6.30 a.m. and invite everybody to join the class virtually. Many of those who cannot join the class on weekdays join it on the mandatory days. On Saturdays and Sundays, the strength of the yoga class is between 50 and 60 participants.

Initially, I used to impart the basics of meditation, yoga, and pranayama to small groups of about 15 people in the conference room of our corporate office on a rotation basis. In our virtual classes, we reserve 15 minutes for pranayama and meditation. The feedback of the participants, particularly those who join us virtually on weekends, has been very positive. They say that they feel better in body and spirit, thanks to yoga and meditation.

The introduction of yoga in the workplace offers multiple benefits. During the online classes, we also discuss related subjects such as nutrition, healthy eating habits, and character building. Adopting a more nutritious diet and practising moderation in alcohol consumption are proven health measures, which we emphasize during our sessions. The employees achieve higher levels of consciousness about the need to be healthy and keep fit. We encourage them to pursue any activity that appeals to them: whether it is meditation and yoga, or a game of badminton or tennis, or jogging or swimming. The idea is to engage in an activity that will contribute towards leading a healthier lifestyle!

I am glad to have led by example in fostering a culture of fitness at Chemline. On special occasions, such as our Foundation Day, we begin the celebrations with a session of yoga and pranayama. For the last few years, the top leaders of our country, inspired by Prime Minister Narendra Modi, have been discovering the benefits of yoga. Not just in India but across the world, the Prime Minister has propagated the message of yoga and even led sessions on International Yoga Day at the United Nations Headquarters as well. We are proud that, at Chemline, we have embraced this secret of maintaining a healthy mind and body for many years.

As a business leader, I can say with confidence that having a healthier workforce is good for the company's balance sheet. If there is a sense of well-being among employees, they are likely to have greater levels of enthusiasm about coming to work. Yoga and meditation are great team-building exercises as well. They foster a sense of kinship and camaraderie among colleagues, creating a feeling of belonging and the belief that they are part of one large family at Chemline. Indirectly, I have noticed that this leads to lower levels of attrition, as employees perceive Chemline to be a happy workplace. They come to their cubicles with a smile on their face, feeling both happy and healthy. With healthier employees, leaves on medical grounds are less frequent.

The participation of employees in our yoga classes is growing every day, and I am sure that a healthier workforce enhances the efficiency and productivity of our company as well. It has been inculcated as an essential tenet in the culture of our organization. I keep telling my colleagues, 'When you leave the office premises, take happiness home with you. Never take any job-related stress back with you.'

The process of working should never lead to stress. Rather, it should create happiness and excitement. Just to illustrate this, I recently interacted with one of my colleagues, who informed me that her mother-in-law was also inspired by our online yoga and meditation classes and that she joins the class along with my colleague. I always encourage them to include their family members in the yoga and meditation class, whenever possible. Getting to know the family members of my colleagues and finding out about their well-being, and sharing tips on wellness with them, helps create a special bond with them by going the extra mile. This is a bond that makes Chemline special for its employees.

Along with practising yoga and pranayama, equally essential is consuming fresh food such as vegetables, fruits, and sprouts. Having too much processed and cooked food—such as chips, pizza, and noodles—as well as excessive chapatis and rice, can lead to many health complications. On a personal level, I begin my day with a nutritious salad comprising both freshly cut fruits and vegetables.

Another very useful practice is fasting, which is an established tradition in most religions of the world. In India, the father of the nation, Mahatma Gandhi, propagated the virtues of fasting. As he wrote in *Young India*: 'Fasting and prayer [...] are a most powerful process of purification [...] A fast to be true must be accompanied by a readiness to receive pure thoughts [...] Similarly, a prayer to be true has to be intelligible and definite.'[6]

The Magic of Vipassana Meditation

For a long time, I was keen to learn Vipassana. Many years ago, I used to watch and appreciate the insightful television lectures on the subject by Satya Narayana Goenka ji. For the uninitiated, Vipassana is a form of meditation that the Buddha rediscovered and practised to attain nirvana. Since childhood, I have had a keen interest in spirituality.

Mr Goenka set up centres around the world to teach Vipassana. It is a 10-day programme, wherein participants must remain silent and also stay away from their digital devices, fully immersing themselves in meditation. I was keen on doing the course, but had failed to identify a time period in which I could switch off my phone.

When a new CEO joined my company in 2023, I decided to stay away from office work for 10 days. Before this, I had never been away from the office for such a long time. Even when I would take a personal leave, I remained in touch with my colleagues and business associates over the phone. I would always check my e-mail and messages and reply to them, and spend one or two hours doing urgent office work.

I selected the Dehradun Centre for my Vipassana training. As soon as I reached the Centre in the afternoon, I was enrolled and given a small room for my stay. All my gadgets and possessions, such as my mobile phone, laptop, diary, and notebook, were deposited with the organizers.

The period of noble silence or *Arya Maun* was to begin at 7 p.m. Arya Maun means silence of body, speech, and mind, in

---

[6]Gandhi, Mahatma, 'Fasting and Prayer', *Young India*, https://tinyurl.com/2v3nurm8. Accessed on 14 May 2025.

which the participants take a vow of noble silence and refrain from speaking, writing, reading, or any other form of communication. It allows the practitioner to turn inward, free from distractions and influences of external communications. The purpose of this silence is to cultivate deep introspection, concentration and insight.

The organizers provided us with a simple *satvik* lunch.[7] This was my first experience of being without a phone or a laptop. I was on my own immediately upon reaching my room. After lunch, I had a good nap and slept for about two hours. I was cut off from the rest of the world—no discussions, meetings or planning sessions. The result was enhanced quality of sleep.

In the evening, at 7 p.m., 100 participants converged in a large hall where we were given an introduction to the course. From the next day onwards, we were to be ready by 4.30 a.m. for the first Vipassana session. Throughout the day, there was a strict routine of *dhyan* or meditation sessions which continued till 9 p.m. There were breaks for breakfast at 6.30 a.m., lunch at 11 a.m., and evening tea and light snacks at 5.30 p.m.

This strenuous 10-day schedule appeared very long to me at times, as I was missing out on the progress of my business. I was counting every passing day. But after 10 days of completion of the course, I felt like a different person—my mind was very quiet and relaxed. Before the course, I used to take mild medicines to regulate my blood pressure. But I was surprised to discover that my BP had returned to normal after completing the course, without any medication.

Having discovered the immense benefits of this meditation process, I wanted to share the Vipassana practice with my colleagues. Therefore, after coming back from the Centre, I conducted a

---

[7]A satvik or sattvic diet is a type of plant-based diet within Ayurveda where food is divided into what is defined as three yogic qualities (guna) known as sattva, some of which include 'pure, essential, natural, vital, energy-containing, clean, conscious, true, honest, wise'.

Vipassana class for my team members at Chemline. There was an enthusiastic response to the course, with about 75 people in attendance. Everyone was very eager to learn Vipassana meditation. Based on this positive feedback from our team, we introduced weekly Vipassana classes at our organization. Our team members find it really interesting and say that they feel relaxed and calm after the meditation sessions. So, along with our weekly yoga classes, which are held every Saturday morning at 7, we have also introduced Vipassana classes on Thursday evenings at 8.

Now, let us look closely at the concept of Vipassana. In Sanskrit and Pali, the word '*pashna*' means 'to see'. The word '*vi*' is short for *vishesh* or special. So, 'Vipassana' means to view everything the way it is—with equanimity, without any attachment or hatred. Gautam Buddha rediscovered this technique around 2,500 years ago.

So, what does one need to do in this technique? Well, put simply, one has to observe one's breath very closely.[8] We have to become alert and conscious of our breath as we inhale and exhale, and also observe the arising and passing of thoughts, sensations, and emotions without feeding the tendency to react or engage with them. From the third day onwards, for one hour, three times a day, the practitioner must remain still in an erect posture, without any movement of the body. For twelve hours every day, the practitioners must engage only in the practice of Vipassana meditation.

Now, let us understand the primary benefits of Vipassana. These include a reduction in stress levels, the quieting of the mind, and acquiring the capabilities of deep study and analysis. Another benefit is acquiring the ability to live in the moment. To sum up, for me, Vipassana means cleansing one's soul by travelling deep inside one's psyche.

---

[8]'How to Sit in Vipassana Meditation: A Comprehensive Guide to Cultivating Inner Peace', *Cymbiotika*, 25 March 2025, https://tinyurl.com/yck7czyb. Accessed on 14 May 2025.

To practise Vipassana meditation, one needs to follow five simple principles, namely:

- Never steal
- Never tell lies
- Never kill living beings
- Never get intoxicated
- Practice *sheel* and *sadachar* (This means being at your best behaviour all the time.)

ISKCON's Global Impact in Promoting India's Heritage

I have a special connection with a few self-help groups and sociocultural organizations. One of these is the International Society for Krishna Consciousness, more commonly known as ISKCON. Remaining in touch with devotees of ISKCON—who are highly qualified and have sacrificed their careers and worldly comforts—always motivated me and kept me away from overindulgence in worldly pleasures.

According to me, ISKCON has achieved two commendable feats. One of these is that they reach out with mid-day meals for schoolchildren, and distribute free food to anybody who needs it in the community. It is a really noble cause, as inspired by their founder, A.C. Bhaktivedanta Swami Prabhupada. The second and more important feat is that they have set up centres worldwide, in every international capital and major city. This is praiseworthy indeed! I can vouch for this from personal experience.

For instance, I mentioned to them that I was planning to travel to the US in September 2023. They immediately helped me get in touch with their colleagues in New York. I spoke to the devotee, and we decided that I would spend some time one evening at the ISKCON temple there. Similarly, when I mentioned to the ISKCON volunteers that I would be going to North Carolina in the US, they helped me coordinate with one devotee there. It wasn't in one country alone, they also promised to help me establish similar contacts with their colleagues in Argentina and Mexico. These initiatives are commendable!

I feel that even in remote corners of the world, the good folks at ISKCON are helping keep Indian tradition and culture alive. Let me share an example of this with you. A few years ago, Chemline was participating in a packaging exhibition at São Paulo, one of the biggest cities in Brazil. I wasn't really expecting it, but an Indian visited us at the stall. After some time, when the rush of customers subsided a little, he spoke to me. He mentioned that he has roots in India and that seeing me in this alien country made him remember his homeland. He chatted with me for some time, and we instantly struck a rapport. The gentleman went on to invite me to have dinner with his family. He said that his wife would prepare home-style Indian food for us. When I tasted the food, it lived up to the promise! Although the taste was not as authentic as we get with Indian spices, I really relished the experience of having homely food so far away from New Delhi, in São Paulo.

After we had dinner, he shared his concern with me. He said that there was no temple in São Paulo. Owing to this, his son had begun visiting the church and had given up on his faith and converted to Christianity. There were hardly any Indians staying there, and there was no sense of community. Before calling it a day, he made two requests to me. One, he said that I should courier a picture or statue of Lord Krishna to him from India. Second, he wanted to get a dhoti, since it was difficult to find one in Brazil, and he liked wearing traditional Indian attire on special occasions and festivals such as Deepawali.

As you can see, one of the greatest contributions of ISKCON is helping fill this vacuum in the lives of Indians living abroad—helping them find a slice of their tradition and religion thousands of miles away from India, and helping preserve their culture and traditions. We don't realize its value here, since we take it for granted in India.

The commendable cause of feeding the hungry has been on since A.C. Bhaktivedanta Swami Prabhupada founded ISKCON in New York in 1965, at the age of 69. The spark that he lit in the West, more than five decades ago, has today turned into a global movement that takes the ethos of Indian-ness and Indian culture forward. At a personal level, ever since I began my association with the organization, they have been a source of inspiration for me. Every year, they visit me on my birth anniversary at my workplace, and involve my colleagues in making my birthday meaningful through their dancing, singing, and prayers, and also by chanting:

Hare Krishna, Hare Krishna,
Krishna Krishna Hare Hare;
Hare Ram Hare Ram
Ram Ram Hare Hare

Whenever I visit their elegantly built temples, whether in India or abroad, I feel a sense of belonging and spirituality that is difficult

to experience elsewhere. For the thousands of people who visit their temples abroad, ISKCON acts as a soul-keeper and provides a connection with their spiritual roots.

How My Spiritual Practices Helped Me Evolve as a Better Human Being

Some family friends introduced my wife to the concept of Japanese Soka Gakkai Buddhism. That is how I met its practitioners when they came to my house. Gradually, I began practising this form of Buddhism, particularly the chanting process that involves repeating the line '*Nam-myoho-renge-kyo*'. I used to chant early in the morning with the group for close to 45 days. Later, I continued to chant on my own.

Recently, during a stressful personal month, I resumed the chanting practice. This time, I chanted in the evening, along with a practitioner who joined me online. I did this for a couple of months. The chanting process helped me tide over a challenging phase and gave me enormous strength.

One of the most beautiful tenets of Buddhism is the sense of community it offers. Say, if one member of the community is facing a problem in their life, every member of the community helps their comrade overcome it. In my own example, the members of the chanting group offered to come home and chant in order to help me. When I was passing through the difficult phase, one hour of chanting along with other members of the community helped empower my mind and purify it.

In case you are in the middle of a really challenging phase and feel helpless, the chanting process empowers you and takes you from a negative mindset to a positive one. I can vouch for this based on my experience! Such is the potential of chanting 'Nam-myoho-renge-kyo' in Soka Gakkai Buddhism. It means that you reap the rewards of whatever you sow. I bow down before the universal law of cause and effect. Everything that's happening to you is a manifestation of your own actions. So, there is no point blaming anyone else.

The best part about Soka Gakkai Buddhism is the strong sense of empathy, community, and camaraderie. Your fellow group members will hold your hand and help you navigate through turbulent waters and will stand with you in a challenging phase. It is of enormous help to anybody in distress. They emphasize that service to society is the best way to accumulate wisdom and peace of mind.

Over the years, I have also explored other ways of meditation and contemplation.

Having experienced the Sudarshan Kriya of Sri Sri Ravi Shankar ji of the Art of Living, I can look back and see the manner in which it helps an individual. The Sudarshan Kriya helps you calm down and elevate the thinking process. For instance, at the individual level, it transformed my personality. Managing a large team wasn't easy for me initially, and I would lose my patience with those who were inefficient in their work. Practising the Sudarshan Kriya helped me become a calmer person. It clarifies your thought process and enables such control over your mind that anger towards others no longer arises.

I have also appreciated the gems of wisdom shared by the Brahma Kumaris spiritual movement. Having attended a two-day course in Gurugram (previously Gurgaon), I gained enormously from the lectures of, among others, their leader Shivani Behn—a practitioner and a teacher of Rajyoga meditation. She talks about resolving particular issues and situations that a person may be facing in their day-to-day life. For instance, in case a person is misbehaving or is rude to you, and you too behave in a similar manner, you only fuel the animosity. Rather, you can perceive their behaviour in another way. This misbehaviour may indicate that the person is disturbed and needs help. You should help the person come out of this state of mind and give them an opportunity to reform themselves. To achieve this, you must work on changing your own point of view.

All these insights into the mind, behavioural science, and spirituality—whether it is from the Japanese Buddhist teachers, Sri Sri Ravi Shankar, or the Brahma Kumaris—have made me a better person and helped me evolve. I may have been a difficult person at one time, but I have changed, and this evolution has helped me enormously. One cannot let difficulties push one into depression or bog one down. All the problems that come one's way are opportunities for self-improvement.

Today, I can look back and say with some degree of satisfaction that I have never let problems in my professional or personal life become insurmountable obstacles. I have overcome them and moved forward on two fronts. As a first-generation entrepreneur, I have built a really successful business venture from scratch and have learnt from my problems and evolved as a person at the same time. I have also developed business principles that I have never compromised, and adapted to my circumstances, welcomed those circumstances and looked for *ananda* or bliss in these very circumstances. I believe in living every moment and enjoying it.

If a person's loved ones, family members, or children are misbehaving with them, one way to perceive it is that the loved ones are deeply upset. One should pray that they achieve peace of mind. The prayer will reach them and help the healing process. I have taken the synthesis of all these philosophies and successfully implemented them in my interactions with my colleagues and family members. As a person, I have made enormous strides. I have stepped out of my comfort zone and discovered comfort in unfamiliar terrain. More than just becoming a successful entrepreneur, I strongly believe progress as a person is far more rewarding and satisfying.

LIFE LESSONS

- Yoga and meditation help you become healthier in both body and mind.
- There is a deep relation between breathing and the mind—when you observe your breath, you go deep inside your own self and purify your mind.
- Silence and meditation can help cure many bodily disorders and diseases, helping one feel restful and calm.
- Yoga and meditation promote team building and contribute to a healthier workforce and workplace.
- A healthier workplace and higher efficiency are always beneficial for business.
- A strong sense of empathy and community is fostered when your fellow group members hold your hand, help you navigate turbulent waters, and stand by you during challenging phases of life.
- Practising the Sudarshan Kriya has helped me become a calmer person. It untangles the thought process and helps you to control your mind.
- From the Brahma Kumaris, I learnt that misbehaviour often indicates that a person is disturbed and needs help. You should assist such individuals in overcoming this state of mind and give them an opportunity to reform themselves.

PART III

Life Is a Laboratory

6

Life Is a Laboratory

This chapter explores how every experience—success, failure, joy, or struggle—serves as an experiment, offering lessons that shape who we are and who we become. Each moment becomes a test tube for growth, discovery, and transformation.

How My Personal Habits Helped Me Become Successful

I keep telling people that they must continuously explore themselves—they should treat life as a laboratory. Just as experiments are conducted in a research laboratory to develop new products, one should keep experimenting in one's own life as well. These experiments might be related to food, sleep, medicines, work, exercise, meditation, reading, friendships, office tasks, daily routines, and so on. That is precisely what I have done throughout my life! Through these experiments, I kept introducing novelties into my life, thus enriching it with excitement.

One way that I have followed this is by consciously taking myself out of my comfort zone. This even finds reflection in my everyday routine. For instance, I bathe in cold water, even when the temperature drops to chilly levels in the winter. I immediately feel invigorated and vibrant afterwards. My friends and well-wishers often worry that I might fall ill if I continue doing this during the cold Delhi winters, but it has now become a habit. My body and mind have adapted to it. Similarly, many of India's yogis and ascetics wear just one piece of clothing or less and venture out in the elements—braving the heat, cold, or rain—in their quest for self-discovery. Never do they complain about feeling too cold or hot.

Let me explain the thought process behind this. I believe that one must be grateful that the Almighty has not put you in any discomfort. But you must step out of your comfort zone yourself, and put your body under a little bit of pressure or expose it to some form of discomfort. So, giving up on the comfort of bathing with hot water is my way of attuning my body to a little bit of discomfort. Similarly, fasting once in a while is not only good for detoxifying our bodies but also for our mental control. These are among the few things that I have experimented with.

Another personal habit that helps me is getting up early every morning—this has been one of the best discoveries that I have made about myself. Even earlier, I used to get up at 5 a.m. But for the last two years, I have got up even earlier at 3.30 or 4 a.m. Since I began doing this, my health has seen a dramatic improvement, and I get time to attempt new things. I remember my great friend, Dilip Salwi, who wrote many books on science and the environment. He used to get up at 2.30 a.m. to write.

What helped me make up my mind about this was a saying by Sadhguru Jaggi Vasudev. In one of his lectures, he explains that for millions of years our body clock was governed by the solar system.[9] It is only in the last 100 years that electric power has been invented. Before that, people's lifestyle was governed by the movement of the sun. Preparation of food for every meal was dependent on the availability of sunlight. When the sun went down, most people went into rest mode. For millions of years, our bodies were used to resting at night. If we follow this age-old wisdom, we can hope to make the most of our day! If you go against it and keep working till late in the night, in a way, you are working against the natural

[9]'Religion, As We Know It, Will Go Down in 100 Years', *Isha Foundation*, 16 June 2016, https://tinyurl.com/y3vwdbf6. Accessed on 11 August 2025.

rhythm of your body, and this works against your health.

Going with this wisdom, I decided to wake up at 4 a.m. every day, and this helped improve my overall health. As an entrepreneur, at times, one is not able to switch off from work at sunset. Still, I make an attempt to complete my office work by 6 p.m. and then spend some time pursuing my passions and hobbies.

Once I reach home, I take an invigorating bath followed by a few minutes of pranayama and prayer. The practice of pranayama gives you high levels of mental relaxation. The next few hours become immensely fruitful and productive once I reach a state of relaxation. I have a really light dinner before calling it a day. I feel that the morning hours are a time when we are at our most healthy and creative best. Earlier, I used to have a bath at 9 a.m., but these days I have a bath early in the morning, before I practise my yoga at 6.30 a.m. By 8 a.m. I have my breakfast and get ready for the day ahead.

After 8 a.m., you have plenty of time to tackle any official or personal engagement. Many people in India begin their day by, 10 a.m. but if I am ready two hours earlier, I get a head start on everybody. Having got up early, between 4 a.m. and 5 a.m., I will have already checked and responded to my e-mail and messages from the previous day. In this way, getting up early sets the tone for the day and helps enhance my personal productivity as well as that of my employees.

One must not make their lifestyles too sedentary. I am a firm believer in the fact that to keep fit, our body must continue to engage in some degree of physical work. This can take the form of jogging, brisk walking or other types of exercise. All these activities enhance aerobic function and blood circulation, thereby helping kick out negativity from a person's mind. For instance, I realized that after the age of 65, running was putting a lot of strain on my knees. Therefore, I stopped running and emphasized a lot more on the practice of yoga. Yoga is an ideal exercise for the entire body. It also raises blood circulation and thereby, helps keep the mind alert and dispels dullness and mental negativity.

Although I had been practising yoga since my childhood, I became a regular practitioner during my college days. During my childhood, we learnt the basics of yoga at an ashram near our residence in Rana Pratap Bagh. As mentioned earlier, our father took us to Dhirendra Brahmachari's Vishwayatan Yogashram in Delhi a few times. Brahmachari was a renowned yoga teacher whose disciples included former Prime Minister Indira Gandhi.

Apart from yoga, I have had the fortune of completing a basic as well as an advanced Art of Living course, taught by the acclaimed guru Sri Sri Ravi Shankar. I found the Sudarshan Kriya course to be enormously beneficial for me. It is an incredible combination of meditation and breathing exercises. The exercise takes the mind into a state that is entirely positive, calm, and creative. It helped me introduce a lot of positive changes in my lifestyle. Subsequently, I practise a short Sudarshan Kriya in the morning. I believe that it is the perfect antidote to mental turbulence and helps one achieve a calmer mind. Taking a cue from my experiences with Sudarshan Kriya and yoga, I have adapted and personalized a routine that works for me. After doing it, I reach a relaxed state of mind. In this state, I begin by forgiving everybody, allowing myself to lead a life free from anxiety.

When I was experiencing a turbulent phase of life, filled with insurmountable problems, I read a book on Sri Sri Ravi Shankar's discourses: Celebrating Silence. In that, he explains a valuable life truth.[10] He says that when you are unhappy and happiness seems far away, you must adopt three principles:

1. 'I am nothing.' This teaches you to do away with *ahankar* or ego.
2. 'I don't need anything.' This will help you reduce your demands on the world.

[10]Sri Sri Ravi Shankar, *Celebrating Silence*, Sri Sri Publications Trust, Delhi, 2008.

3. 'I am here for service.' This will change your attitude towards your own duties vis-à-vis the world.

Adopting these three principles is the key to happiness. And this is the true art of living!

At the physical level, following my routine has improved the quality of my sleep. I get sound, uninterrupted sleep close to eight hours. I am careful about what I eat. While ensuring adequate nutrition, I have one major meal at lunch, along with light meals for breakfast and dinner. In fact, I ensure I never go to sleep with a heavy stomach.

Another enjoyable part of my lifestyle is the hobbies that I have. These include drawing and painting, which are my rediscovered passions, and playing the harmonium. I practise some ragas and Om *dhwani* for about 15 minutes every day, and edit the poetry that I have written. I have also begun getting some formal training in painting and interacting with several artists and painters. I like to be surrounded by greenery; therefore, the Chemline factory premises have a good assortment of shaded trees and plants. It has spawned an ecosystem with some birds and wildlife as well. I want to remain close to nature, not just at home, but even at my workplace. The Chemline factory is a sort of resort surrounded by gardens and forests.

Pursuing this lifestyle enhances the personal efficiency of a person, and this optimum use of time ultimately finds a reflection in the bottom line of a business. Getting a head start of a few hours because of waking up early ensures that I don't directly plunge into the implementation of business goals. I have an additional two or three hours to think about the direction that my business is taking, and I can plan my workflow for the day accordingly. As they say, time is money. Getting up early helps me correct the direction of my life and ultimately makes for good business as well.

Work: The Antidote for Despair

The way bees keep accumulating honey for their future, and then humans take away the output of their hard work–life is very unpredictable for every living being. Human beings, too, keep investing for a rainy day in the hopes of creating a brighter future, but the uncertainties of life can turn all their plans topsy-turvy. Still, as is human nature, hope springs eternal!

My mantra in life is to keep moving forward without looking back. The past and future are only illusions. One has to come out of the influence of the past to infuse a refreshing new energy into life. As I have grown older, I have realized one fact—my imagination is still very young, despite my progressing age. My drive and active mind ensure that I set up two new projects every year, and this means that I am inviting more work and longer working hours for myself.

Remaining busy helps you come out of the influence of the past and also helps you work towards enjoying the present. This, in turn, is the mantra for a brighter future. When we immerse ourselves in work, we forget the agonizing memories of the past. We keep working in the present, and a little bit for the future. This makes the quality of life better. As the iconic author and Nobel Prize winner Ernest Hemingway, considered to be one of the best novelists of the twentieth century, has observed: 'Work could cure almost anything.'

The Golden Hour: The Need to Develop Personal Habits for Profound Living

To have knowledge is one thing; to apply it, experiment with it, and discover its benefits and drawbacks is quite another. As a trained scientist, I have cultivated a temperament that embraces scientific reasoning and a spirit of experimentation. There may be a lot of people with great academic qualifications, such as MPhil and PhDs,

but very few who *apply* the same knowledge to their own lives.

I believe I am applying knowledge for the benefit of my career, health, and life, and also for the benefit of the people around me. I do not simply follow the tried and tested methods; I experiment with one aspect of knowledge and see whether it is working or not, and then go on to repeat the entire process. I have arrived at my own conclusions only by doing and experiencing. This is what I have done throughout my life.

I have found inspiration in what Sadhguru Jaggi Vasudev so beautifully describes as 'profoundly experiencing your life'. Suppose, on average, you sleep for 8 hours and spend another 4 hours getting ready and having meals, etc. This means that your machine needs 50 per cent of the day's 24 hours for maintenance, which means it is not very efficient. Going by these hypotheses, if you have lived 80 years, you have experienced just 40 of them. The rest of the time you have spent on routine chores without experiencing anything. To experience life more profoundly, you have to use time creatively and purposefully—without frittering away and indulging in wasteful thinking.

If you want to experience life profoundly, with depth, you require more waking and creative hours. These days, I am working towards experimenting on ways to glean more and more waking and creative hours from my everyday routine. I believe that this will enable me to achieve a greater in-depth experience of life.

Let me tell you how I am working towards it. Five years ago, my routine was such that I used to go for a walk and practice yoga at about 7.30 a.m. after waking up at 5 a.m. I realized I ended up wasting time discussing trivial topics with people in the park, after a leisurely walk and yoga. It was a complete waste of time. I realized I had to break that routine and come out of it. Today, I think that although going out in the morning is a healthy habit, it is not the most productive use of time. Now, instead of spending two hours in the park, I practise yoga for one hour on my balcony. Also, earlier I used to spend about 15–20 minutes relaxing after a yoga session before I had my bath. Now, I save this time and have a bath before my yoga practice. I have again saved another 20 minutes, which would instead be spent in lethargy. As a result, I find more time to pursue activities that I find meaningful.

Even at the weekend, when many people might bathe at noon, I have already enjoyed my cup of tea and read the newspaper by 7.45 a.m. By the early hours, I have finished bathing and saying my prayers, leaving me more time to discover what is happening around the world in a non-rushed, relaxed manner. Spending three days a week at my factory premises minimises travel time—every small thing makes a difference.

With minor modifications to my personal routine, I have managed to conserve close to two hours in the morning. This time is utilized in purposeful living and experiencing life profoundly. The quantum of my work has more than doubled these days. To gain the additional time required to tackle these new tasks, I have to return to make tweaks to my lifestyle. So, if it means having dinner at 7 p.m., I am ready for it.

A concept being propagated by many exponents of time management, wellness, and life coaches is that of 'the golden hour', or the first hour before sunrise. In our scriptures, too, it finds honourable mention as the '*Brahma muhurat*'. In a book written by Brian Spear, *The Golden Hour: A 3-Step Morning Routine to Unlock Your Energy, Boost Performance, and Beat Burnout*, the emphasis of the author, a transformative coach is upon providing concrete steps to incorporate daily habits that promote well-being and individual health, and help you conserve a precious hour of your personal time.[11] For me, the biggest takeaways from the book were learning how to view mornings from an entirely new perspective, developing and nurturing self-care practices that begin in the morning and continue throughout the day to produce powerful results, and establishing a structured morning routine framework.

▪

The old chestnut of wisdom about dietary habits, in which it was said that one should 'breakfast like a king, lunch like a prince, and dine like a beggar' does need some modification, at least according to what I have experienced and experimented with. Many health proponents recommend long hours on an empty stomach, as it

[11]Spear, Brian, *The Golden Hour: A 3-Step Morning Routine to Unlock Your Energy, Boost Performance, and Beat Burnout*, 2021.

works towards the detoxification of your body.[12]

After reading the opinion of Dr Biswaroop Roy Chowdhury, who advocates consuming a significant quantity of raw fruits and vegetables in one's total food intake, I experimented with the same and found that it considerably improved my health.[13] As we know, it is only human beings who consume cooked food; the rest of the animal kingdom eats it in its natural, raw state. So, I incorporated raw fruits and vegetables into my everyday diet. As an experiment, I started having vegetable and fruit salad, along with sprouted beans, for breakfast, as the first light meal of the day. I season it with some salt, chaat masala, and also a bit of honey. Sometimes, I also add mint chutney to the salad, which makes for a tasty and good breakfast. I also enjoy a cup of masala tea sweetened with jaggery after some time, while reading my morning newspaper.

I have also eliminated onion and garlic from my meals. When some of his disciples asked Sadhguru whether leaving out garlic was a good idea, as it is a repository of food with medicinal properties, he gave a brilliant explanation, saying: 'Yes, it is medicinal. But do you take medicine every day?'[14] Leaving out garlic and onion, as I have discovered, has multiple benefits. The first is restoration of the original aroma and flavour of food, which is often overpowered by the pungent aroma of garlic, for example. Those who have meals at my place cannot stop praising its flavour and taste. Whenever any of my friends asks me how this taste has been achieved, I tell them that there is no secret recipe but that I have just cut out the garlic that used to block the original flavour of the grains and vegetables, which are a mainstay of most vegetarian meals.

---

[12] 'Health Tips from Sadhguru', *Sadhguru Wisdom*, https://tinyurl.com/yptpmz6x. Accessed on 11 August 2025.

[13] 'DIP Diet: Reverse Lifestyle Diseases Naturally', *DIP Diet*, https://tinyurl.com/4drfv73e. Accessed on 11 August 2025.

[14] 'Eliminate These 5 Foods That Harm Your Body! As per Sadhguru's Diet Plan', *Masala Monk*, 14 June 2023, https://tinyurl.com/3xhn8p2v. Accessed on 11 August 2025.

At lunch time I again have a sizeable portion of salad, lentils, a green vegetable cooked in Indian style, and one millet chapati. This is my major meal of the day. After lunch, I squeeze in a power nap of 10–15 minutes before I resume my routine. I feel refreshed and energized to take on the tasks at work. At dinner, once again, I have salad, along with a specially prepared vegetable soup without grinding the vegetables. I've been following this food routine for the last two years and have experienced enormous health benefits because of this.

Your existence in this world is because of this body—if the body and mind are not there, you will cease to exist. If your body and mind are healthy, you can experience this world in a better, more profound manner. So first and foremost, it is important that we keep our body and mind healthy and happy. In a way, the body is a kind of clothing for our soul. If we burden this soul with very heavy clothing, the soul will be weighed down. So, we must give this soul the lightest clothing possible. So, the first thing is to reduce one's weight if you are obese.

Over a period of time, I have discovered that eating raw fruits and vegetables has a curative effect. A number of lifestyle diseases can be prevented by eating raw fruits and vegetables, along with the regulation of sugar levels and blood pressure.[15] Weight reduction was an additional benefit as well. When your body is lighter, you feel more energetic, and it helps control your blood pressure, sugar and other vital health parameters.

At the age of 72, if I can become healthier, energetic, and extend my working hours—thanks to the simple recipe of tweaking my personal habits, making my food nutritious and tastier, along with consuming less medicines—what else can one wish for? I believe I am in the middle of a highly productive phase of my life. Suppose I live another 'x' years, I will experience profound living equivalent to another '1.5x' years. That is a resolution worth looking forward to!

---

[15]'What Is the Raw Food Diet?', *UCLA Health*, 22 April 2025, https://tinyurl.com/5atwhcnv. Accessed on 14 May 2025.

Follow the Sun: How to Create Living Spaces Full of Positivity

I think a good way of feeling creative, more energetic, and optimistic towards the future is to stay in a home full of natural light. If a lot of sunlight enters your room directly, and you are able to see greenery all around you, your health levels improve, your creativity multiplies, and so do your achievements. The place where you sit in your living room must also be well-ventilated, with an abundance of fresh, unpolluted air.

If the air quality and natural light are good, you can certainly multiply your health levels, quality of life, and your life expectancy. I believe one must plan one's living spaces in great detail to ensure a good supply of clean air, greenery, and plenty of sunshine. On the other hand, if your living spaces are devoid of ventilation, natural light, and greenery, it will have a negative impact on your physical and psychological health.

The availability of sunlight uplifts your mood. There are a number of scientific studies that establish the connection between your mental health and lack of sunlight.[16] Parts of Sweden and Norway are within the Arctic Circle and experience round-the-clock darkness during the winter months. But the 'winter blues', or full-blown seasonal affective disorder, is a problem for many of the residents. Similar complaints about the dark and wet English weather can be heard from those who migrate to the UK from other nations that are full of sunlight.

Lack of sunlight is thought to cause a drop in serotonin levels, contributing to depressed feelings, particularly during winter. These days, when many of us lead mechanical lifestyles, what we miss the most is sunlight. India is blessed to have a variety of seasons; natural beauty of the mountains, rivers, and the sea; and ample sunlight, unlike many countries of Europe and other continents in which sunbathing is a luxury. We are fortunate to get direct

---

[16]Wang, Jie, Zhen Wei, Nan Yao, Caifeng Li, and Long Sun, 'Association Between Sunlight Exposure and Mental Health: Evidence from a Special Population Without Sunlight in Work', *Risk Management and Healthcare Policy*, Vol. 16, 2023, 1049–1057, https://doi.org/10.2147/RMHP.S420018; Kent, Shia T., Leslie A. McClure, William L. Crosson, Donna K. Arnett, Virginia G. Wadley, and Nalini Sathiakumar, 'Effect of Sunlight Exposure on Cognitive Function Among Depressed and Non-depressed Participants: A REGARDS Cross-sectional Study', *Environmental Health*, Vol. 8, 2009, 34, https://doi.org/10.1186/1476-069X-8-34. Both accessed on 14 May 2025.

sunlight throughout the year. Parts of India are harnessing the power of solar energy to great effect. Therefore, there is no reason we cannot make sunlight and greenery a part of our lives.

When I discovered that most people are suffering from a deficiency of Vitamin D, I decided to invest in making my living space full of sunlight and also full of greenery. When I do yoga on my balcony in the early morning, I get the maximum benefit from direct exposure to sunlight. It is no surprise that the Surya Namaskar is an important routine in the discipline of yoga, which originated in our country.

Having plants in the house has a relaxing impact on your mind and improves creativity. My home is open from all four directions and has rooms that receive sunlight during sunrise as well as sunset. Reddish orange, yellow, white, and blue colours of the rising and setting sun have a profound impact on me. The colours are beautiful and mesmerizing. I love to observe and feel the movements of the sun, and have done a number of paintings of the same. Therefore, we decided to document this passion of mine by creating a corporate calendar that has images of the rising and setting sun.

You can achieve the benefits of natural ventilation by using the structure of the building to allow the maximum flow of air. People must understand that wherever they sit in their living space—whether it is their living room, workstation, or bedroom—it must be well-ventilated. If that is not so, and you sit in an enclosed space, gradually the levels of fresh air will reduce.

Many of us work in corporate environments equipped with air conditioning or heating, where there is no replenishment of fresh air. Over time, this can lead to elevated levels of carbon dioxide and other indoor pollutants. As a result, we end up breathing stale indoor air, which can contribute to discomfort, reduced cognitive performance, and, in some cases, a higher risk of respiratory issues. If you work outdoors, the rising pollution levels in our cities can be dangerous for your lungs and other organs. Therefore, the importance of having well-ventilated rooms filled with filtered, fresh air cannot be overemphasized. If your oxygen intake is higher because of good air quality, it will ultimately help enhance your life expectancy.

LIFE LESSONS

- I am a firm believer that, to keep fit, our bodies must engage in some degree of physical activity. So step out of your comfort zone.
- For millions of years, our bodies have been accustomed to resting after sunset. By following this age-old wisdom, we can hope to make the most of our day.
- As they say, time is money. Rising early helps me steer my life in the right direction and, ultimately, makes for good business as well.
- Remaining busy helps you move on from the past and enjoy the present.
- When we immerse ourselves in work, we forget the agonizing memories of the past. This improves the quality of life.
- If you are not using your time creatively and working purposefully, and instead are frittering it away in wasteful thinking, you are not truly experiencing life.
- If your living spaces are devoid of ventilation, natural light, and greenery, it will have a negative impact on your physical and psychological health.

7

Travel Is a Teacher

Every journey leaves behind more than memories; it imparts lessons no classroom can teach. Travel broadens horizons, challenges assumptions, and shapes perspectives, making the world our greatest teacher.

Travels Around the Globe

During one of my travels, I found myself sitting with a seasoned and highly successful person. He was 85 years old. I asked him, 'What is the secret of your success? And what is the secret of your good health that, even at this age, you remain so active?' His reply was, 'I keep travelling, and that keeps me very healthy.'

When a businessperson travels to exotic lands and cities to sell their products, they come across a wide variety of people and cultures. The experience of discovering new societies and witnessing different cultures and ways of doing business is a big learning process. When you come across different companies, you realize that their way of manufacturing products and managing their workforce and capital resources may be very different from what you had envisaged. There is so much to learn from each other's systems and cultures, particularly through the cross-pollination of ideas.

Let me recount how I bagged the first export deal for Chemline at the turn of the century. In 2001, I travelled to the United Arab Emirates (UAE) for the first time. The cleanliness, the imposing skyscrapers, and the glitz and glamour of Dubai left me impressed.

I was surprised to see a lot of Indian expats in the airports, malls and offices of the UAE.

My host picked me up from my hotel, and we proceeded to his office for a sit-down meeting to discuss business. Impressed by Chemline's credentials and product mix, our host, the CEO of the company, expressed interest in placing his first order. The discussion eventually led to quality and pricing. It was then that he asked me about the price we would charge for a container shipment. At that time, I had very little idea about the prevailing prices in the UAE. Looking at the products, and on the basis of the knowledge that most of their imports were from Europe, I spontaneously decided to take a gamble. I told them, 'I really want to initiate business with you. So, you can pay me 15 per cent less than what you pay the current suppliers.' My counterpart immediately agreed and showed me the existing bills. I realized that the price was almost twice the prevailing price in India.

That is how I clinched my first overseas deal for Chemline!

On most of my visits abroad, I have seen that the standards of work are higher there. Many times, I have tried to implement these systems and ways of work back home in India—to usher in that organizational culture in our settings. Travel is the greatest teacher one can hope for. I wish to call this learning the 'Graduation from the University of Hard Knock'. Many times, when you take a late-night red-eye flight, you gear up to work in that style and train your body to battle jet lag and work in different time zones, thereby enhancing your productivity.

In this way, travel keeps you young and energetic. In May 2023, when I visited Moscow and Riyadh, I felt this more than ever. One of the Chemline teams met me in Russia, and another team joined me in Saudi Arabia. I was the only constant team member in both legs of our long journey. I checked out of my hotel in Moscow at 8 a.m. and reached Riyadh close to midnight. After 16 hours of travelling, I knew I had to honour all my meeting commitments.

In the light of the conflict with Ukraine, Russia has been deprived of materials that were being supplied by European countries. We wanted to convert our visit to Moscow into a big business opportunity for Chemline. We sensed the vacuum in the industrial supplies in Moscow, and wanted to play our role in filling that gap. Even as many companies have exited the Russian market in the aftermath of the conflict with Ukraine, many others have found ways to enter the same market. India has, in recent times, been one of Russia's major trading partners. Our partnership has strengthened across many sectors, including energy and oil cooperation.

It is an opportunity not just for Chemline, but also for many other enterprises across different industrial segments. Our partners in Russia are looking forward to investors and entrepreneurs from other countries, particularly India. This is a sentiment that I felt was gaining ground during my visit. I noticed that the levels of automation have enhanced to a great extent in their businesses since my last visit to the country. Compared to Russia, our work processes are still labour-intensive to a large extent. In terms of standards of living and the indices related to them, India has a lot of catching up to do with Russia.

When I had a free day in Moscow, I indulged in an immensely interesting creative pursuit. I visited a painting exhibition at one of the premier art galleries in the Russian capital, where the works of the country's greatest painters were displayed across 70 halls. I was really happy to spend nearly four hours exploring the gallery, especially as I had recently revived my childhood hobby of painting. It was a great learning experience to witness the works of Russian masters; truly, a day well spent!

During my visit to the gallery, I purchased a few paintings, sketchbooks, bags, and replicas of the Russian masters who caught my imagination. I visited a few shops that dealt with these art-related merchandise. Unfortunately, while hopping from one shop to another, I left behind a bag full of art merchandise at one of them, and subsequently returned to my hotel. It was only after I had reached my room that I realized that my purchases had been left behind at the first shop. As I was really tired, I went to sleep. The next morning, I had a flight to catch and informed the hotel reception about the situation. The receptionist assured me that she would speak to the shop and confirm whether my bag had indeed been left behind there. She promised that in case it was found, she would personally visit the shop and get the things back to the hotel.

Three days later, after I returned to India, I got a call from the hotel. The receptionist called me and informed me that my bag had indeed been found! 'Dr Goel, I have got your things back to the hotel,' she said. My things were lying safely at the shop, just as I had left them. I then asked my business associate to collect them from the hotel and courier them to me. That is the kind of honesty in public life that Russians display, and I feel it is highly inspiring and something that we can learn from them.

This was also not the first time I have experienced this honesty. Once, I left a very expensive pen somewhere. That evening, the pen came back to my room after somebody discovered it in the hotel premises. Not just honesty in public life, but the work ethic is superior whether one travels to China, Europe, or the US. This is most evident in the services sector—in malls, marketplaces, and everywhere where the willingness to serve is needed. I believe, as a nation, we have some catching up to do in this regard.

On the positive side, in the last few years, there has been a big shift in the perception of Indians who travel abroad for work or for pleasure. I felt this more than ever on my most recent trip to Russia and Saudi Arabia. We had participated in an exhibition called the 'Saudi Print & Pack 2023'. During the exhibition, strangers would walk up to me and say that India is rising as opposed to China. 'India up, China down' was a common conversation starter in Riyadh. Our image has been enhanced manifold ever since the BJP (Bharatiya Janata Party) government, led by Prime Minister Narendra Modi, came to power in 2014. Even our neighbours realize this.

Let me share an anecdote with you. As mentioned before, we

had participated in an exhibition in Riyadh. One time, during this exhibition, a Pakistani national visited our stall. He introduced himself as the regional manager of a leading company based in Riyadh. Initially, he was a little reticent, but over time, he began chatting with me. When I inquired about the business environment in Pakistan, he said that things were really bad. So much so that he was reluctant to return to Pakistan on a regular basis. He also said that there were many people who approached him for assistance during his visits, as he was perceived as a prosperous expat employee based in Riyadh. His final words to me were: 'Pakistan must merge with India the way East Germany and West Germany united.'

We are the fifth largest economy, and by the end of the decade, we will become the third largest. Under Prime Minister Modi, India's image has shot up as the fastest-growing large economy, and this is evident when one steps out of the country. If our work ethic matches our economic growth and the speed of infrastructure creation, India has the potential to become a leader on the world map in a really short time.

Travels in the Indian Subcontinent

Some would perceive travelling to clients or living out of a suitcase as an occupational hazard for entrepreneurs. But unlike many other CEOs, who get exhausted with meetings and business trips, I've enjoyed the travel immensely. Additionally, it makes for good business! Whenever I have visited a factory in a remote part of the country and explained our product to them, they went on to become Chemline customers for life. Being an inveterate traveller, I looked forward to these trips.

I recall flying to Bagdogra in 1992 and heading to Sikkim by road from there to visit the brewery of celebrated actor Danny Denzongpa at Yuksom. I saw Danny's original modest home as well, from where he had progressed to become such a famous actor and businessman. Despite her son's celebrity status, his mother was

still staying in a small home at the time. In 2003, Denzongpa was awarded the Padma Shri—India's fourth-highest civilian honour.

Along with being an actor, he had also set up a brewery business in Sikkim. Today, his company owns three breweries in Sikkim, Assam, and Odisha. Yuksom Breweries also acquired a brewery in Assam, Rhino Agencies. I am proud of my business association with Yuksom. We have been supplying them for more than two decades now.

Unlike many other states in the region, Sikkim has a highly evolved home-grown industrial ecosystem. The pristine environs of the state, pure unpolluted water, and emphasis on organic farming have also spawned a thriving pharmaceutical and spirits business there. Today, Yuksom Breweries is one of the highest tax-paying companies in Sikkim, contributing more than ₹100 crore annually to the state.[17]

As I was fond of travelling, I mixed my passion for exploring new places with business development. On that same trip to Sikkim in 1992, I was really impressed with the natural beauty and cleanliness of Gangtok, its capital, where I stayed in a hotel. I remember taking several pictures of Rangpo River—a tributary of the Teesta, which demarcates the border between the Pakyong district of Sikkim and the Kalimpong district of West Bengal. Located on a hilltop nearby is Sikkim Distilleries. The beautiful setting of this distillery is a sight I will remember for a long time! It was located at such a high altitude that I felt like I was walking among clouds. Once I reached, it began to rain and the distillery was enveloped with clouds, which resembled large grey-and-white curtains. Another highlight of the trip was being hosted for a meal and tea party organized by Zanzing Denzongpa, Danny Denzongpa's brother, at a picturesque garden.

Yet another highly enjoyable experience was travelling to Nepal, and then undertaking a road trip from Nepal to Siliguri, West Bengal. I remember travelling from Kathmandu to Lalitpur, and from there to Siliguri—it was a beautiful drive. What caught my eye was the architecture of the houses alongside the highway, made primarily of wood. The ground floor was kept aside for cattle, and the residents stayed on the floors above.

I also remember visiting Phuentsholing, a border town in southern Bhutan. It adjoins the Indian town of Jaigaon, where

---

[17]'Jackie Shroff Launches Three New Products of Yuksom Breweries', *Sikkim Express*, 13 September 2022, https://tinyurl.com/4x8yjh48. Accessed on 8 August 2025.

cross-border trade has resulted in a thriving local economy. A distillery here is also one of the clients of Chemline. I am proud of the fact that we are the preferred partner in a number of countries in the Indian subcontinent, including Nepal, Bhutan, Myanmar, Bangladesh, and Sri Lanka.

Whether it is the verdant valleys of northeast India or Nepal, or the lush greenery and backwaters of Kerala—near the Cherthala suburb in Alappuzha—I look at these visits with fondness and a hint of nostalgia. I have made some lifelong friends in these places and created some unforgettable memories. When I first visited Cherthala, I was mesmerized by the natural beauty and serene setting of the backwaters adjacent to the Vembanad Lake. It had a calming effect on my nerves, and I sat there and kept looking at the backwaters for a few minutes.

At Cherthala, I met the business unit head of United Distilleries for the first time, and we immediately established a rapport based on mutual respect. He later went on to become a senior functionary at Shaw Wallace and continued to assist me and my company. Another pleasant discovery during my travels in South India was a button mushroom unit in the Nilgiri Hills, set up by Ponds India Limited. We travelled to Ooty via Coimbatore to reach the facility. The mushrooms cultivated there were packed in cans, and our glue proved useful to the company for affixing labels around them.

Life indeed has been an adventure, and I have learnt the art of mixing business with pleasure. As India is racing towards becoming a developed country over the next decade, the promise of growth opportunities for the next generation is seen to be enormous. It is my heartfelt desire that this book will provide the required impetus to the next generation of youth to experience success in life and drive the nation forward.

LIFE LESSONS

- Travel is the greatest teacher.
- Learn from the systems and cultures of other countries, as this can foster the cross-pollination of ideas.
- India must learn from the work ethic of developed countries. Combined with our business acumen and demographic dividend, this would create an unbeatable combination.
- Respect for India and for Indians travelling abroad is growing in the eyes of the world.

8
Importance of Family Values

My personal life was quite turbulent. Despite all the challenges in my personal life, I worked hard to make my professional life a success.

With the advent of modernization and economic growth, husband–wife relationships and family values are becoming diluted, and divorce rates are going up in the Indian society. There are now more separated families and children from broken homes, with single parents who are unable to provide proper guidance.

In this chapter, I have included some of my personal experiences and suggestions that may help individuals or families facing similar circumstances. When I encountered personal challenges, I always sought help and guidance, but such support was not available to me.

▪

You would never harm a person you love. If you keep children away from their father or mother, do you truly love them? By cutting a child off from a natural relationship and compelling them to remain incomplete, you deprive them of emotions that only a father or mother can evoke—that of love, respect, and security.

I always tell my children, 'Your mother is the best person in the world.' When my daughter re-established contact with me after 33years, she said that she wanted to relive all the years that she had stayed away from me. These were the emotions she had been nurturing for all these years! Children of broken homes struggle to create stable relationships as adults, which poses challenges in establishing their own relationships. In India, generally, separated spouses do not stay friendly with each other.

This need not always be the case in other parts of the world. Let me illustrate this with an example from my life. A few years ago, I travelled to Sweden to meet a business associate. Since I had arrived in Stockholm in the morning, the plan was that I would invite him over to my hotel for a meeting, to be followed by lunch. As a reciprocal gesture, my friend was planning to take me out for dinner that night. This programme had been agreed upon many weeks before I reached Sweden's cosmopolitan capital.

My friend arrived with his son-in-law at about 11 a.m., and we had a fruitful discussion followed by a sumptuous lunch. During lunch, my friend said, 'Dr Goel, I am sorry. I know I had invited you over for dinner, but I have a personal engagement. I had completely forgotten—it is my daughter's birthday today.' After some time, he added, 'Why don't you join us for the birthday party?' I graciously agreed, and once I reached the venue, I realized the birthday was a little complicated. 'It is the birthday of my daughter from my first wife, with whom I separated more than 20 years ago,' explained my host.

He was a few years older than me at the time of the visit. The son-in-law who had accompanied him was the husband of his daughter from his first wife. He had two children from his second wife as well. His first wife joined us at the birthday party, along with her partner. What I observed at the party was the lack of rancour between former partners, even after they had parted ways. Even the children were okay with each of their separated parents and their respective partners. There was an air of acceptance and equanimity, and very little ill-feeling towards their parents who had divorced or remarried. I was very happy to see this and felt like this is something that we can learn from their society.

Iconic investor Warren Buffett, one of the richest men in the world, and his first wife have displayed no bitterness even after he remarried. In fact, both his partners share a beautiful and understanding relationship. In my personal life, I would ideally want to stay friends with my former spouse and ensure that my children and I enjoy a healthy and friendly relationship. I believe that there should not be too much negativity and baggage associated with separation and divorce.

Another experience I want to share is about the mental health issues that a person who undergoes separation can experience. As discussed previously, the first time I got divorced, I suffered from serious depression and anxiety attacks, and it took me a lot of time and effort to come out of it. The bond that one shares with one's parents comes from a deep sense of love. Notwithstanding how much one argues with one's parents or takes them for granted, one comes back to live with them and into one's comfort zone during tough times. But the dynamics with your life partner are different. You cannot take your wife or husband for granted. The relationship with the spouse evolves gradually and can become relatively delicate. Therefore, these relationships have to be handled carefully.

Mindsets of those in a marriage are shifting these days. These days, partners think they have an alternative. Separation and divorce are becoming an easy option in the realm of social acceptance. The trust factor in the man–woman relationship is reducing, which is why rates of divorce are rising in every society, including India.

Looking at the big picture, in the event of a divorce, we must not keep children deprived of the love of one parent and we need to seriously contemplate the concept of joint parenting. Separation or divorce need not always mean that the husband and wife cannot remain friends. They may not be sharing the same roof or home, but they can still share a warm rapport. The children must not suffer the consequences of differences cropping up among parents. Joint parenting will always work for the benefit of the child. The growth and development that children can achieve if nurtured by both parents cannot be compared to that of a single parent.

▪

After re-establishing contact with me, my daughter inquired about my well-being and asked me whether I was happy. 'I convert every situation into an opportunity and enjoy every moment. That's the principle of my life,' I told her. When we resumed our conversations, she realized the kind of genuine person I am. She told me, 'Papa, you are such a positive person. The only dream I had was to meet my father. Today, that dream has been accomplished. I don't want anything else from my life now.'

On her thirty-eighth birthday, my daughter asked me to pen a poem for her as a gift. This is what I wrote for her.

३८वें जन्म दिवस पर

तुम अब मेरे जीवन का
एक काल्पनिक रेफ़्रेन्स बिंदु हो।
एक बिंदु जहां से सोचता हूँ मैं,
एक बिंदु जहाँ से खुद का मूल्याँकन करता हूँ मैं
एक धुरी हो तुम,
एक क़ब्ज़ा जिस पर घूमता है दरवाज़ा।

तुम ज़िंदगी के इस सफ़र में,
हो मेरा कुछ सामान,
जो खो गया था, छिन गया था,
वह मिल गया मुझे वर्षों पश्चात्।

तुम जिसे मैं कल्पना में मिलने का प्रयत्न करता,
जिसे मैं शून्य में ढूँढता रहता,
जिसे छूने का प्रयत्न करता,
जो केवल यादों के अहसास में थे मेरे साथ
जो केवल धुँधला सा बिम्ब था
मेरे मनह पटल पर, वह मिल गया मुझे आज।
चेहरा तुम्हारा, लगता है अपना सा।
क्या क्या नहीं देखा
इस चेहरे में।
कभी माँ का बिम्ब देखता हूँ,
तो कभी आँखो में खुद को महसूस करता हूँ

जैसे मैं खुद तुममें हूँ।
पूरा परिवार तो झलकता है तुममें
कहा गया वह वैक्यूम, वह ख़ालीपन, वह एकाकीपन,
ये अहसास व ये शब्द,
दूर हो गये मेरे जीवन से।

बहुत कुछ, जो मेरी ज़िंदगी में
अभी भी लुप्त है;
महसूस नहीं करता उसे, वह रिक़्त स्थान
जैसे तुमने कहीं भर दिया हो।
वह रिक्तता, महसूस नहीं करता अब।
मेरे राहें कही आसान कर दी तुमने।
जो केवल कहीं दिल के कोने में था,
आज वह साथ है मेरे।
बातें कर सकता हूँ मैं उससे
उतना ही चाहता है वह भी मुझे,
जितना चाहता हूँ मैं उसको।
क्या है तुम्हारे व मेरे बीच में?
एक ईश्वर का दिया सम्बंध, शाश्वत रहने वाला एक सम्बंध।

आज पूरे ३८ वर्ष हो गए
जब ईश्वर ने भेजा था तुम्हें मेरे घर में।
परंतु, पाँच वर्ष पश्चात बिछड़ गए हम।
३३ वर्ष पश्चात्, आज फिर साथ साथ हैं हम।
क्योंकि, कोई चाहने वाला मिलता है नसीब से

बेटी मिलती है नसीब से, पिता मिलता है नसीब से।

अब साथ साथ ही रहेंगे हम।
अब साथ साथ ही रहेंगे हम।

३८ वाँ जन्म दिन मुबारक हो तुम्हें।

On your 38th birthday

You've become an imaginary reference point in my life—a place from which I evaluate myself.

You are an axis, a foundation on which this door revolves.

In the journey of life, you are the luggage I once lost—
snatched away from me,
Many years later, I have found it again.

You are someone I searched for in the vacuum of my mind,
someone I was with only in my memories,
someone who was just a faint impression on my psyche.
Today, I've found that person.
Your face looks like mine.
I have discovered so many things in that face—
at times, I see a reflection of your mother,
at other times, I see myself reflected in your eyes.
As if I can find myself in your face,
the entire family finds itself reflected there.

Where has that emptiness gone?
That loneliness, those unspoken feelings, those words—
they have left my life.
So much that was once missing,
I no longer feel its absence.

In a way, you have filled that void.
I don't feel that emptiness any longer,
You have made my passage easier,
Something that was once only at the corner of my heart
is now with me today.

Now I can talk to that person,
And that person loves me as much as I love them.
What is this bond between us?
A relationship gifted by the Almighty,
a bond that is eternal.

Today marks 38 years since God sent you into my life—
Yet five years later, we were separated.

Thirty three years on, we are reunited.

Because one is fortunate to have a loved one,
fortunate to have a daughter,
fortunate to have a father.

Now, we will always be together—
always together.

Happy 38th birthday!

As we continued to stay in touch, my daughter would ask me about all the years that she had missed with me. 'Papa, why didn't you come to see me all these years?'

I replied to her with these words, 'Beta, I was suffering from enormous trauma. When I missed you for two years continuously after you went away, I could not lead a normal life. For those two years, I felt so much trauma of separation that cannot be described in words. I wanted to lead a healthy life and stay alive. To come out of that trauma, I destroyed everything that reminded me of my family and loved ones. I could not visit you or meet you because I didn't want to take that risk—what if my emotions had gotten the better of me when I met you? How would I control it? I could no longer live with you and your mother. I couldn't afford to be gripped by emotions again and be unable to do anything about it. King Dasharatha could not cope with separation from his son, Lord Rama, and this led to his death.'

At that time, the anxiety over separation from loved ones had pushed me into depression and led to many health problems. Over time, the layers of time lent a healing touch. Added below are a few poems I wrote after many years of my separation from my family. These poems reflect my emotions about my kids. These emotions are deeply embedded and alive in me. This is how human beings are, and I am one of them.

यादें

कितनी परतें बिछ गईं समय की...
यादें दब गईं...इन परतों के बोझ तले...
फिर भी...कभी कभी...उभर आती...
समय की परतों को चीरती,
दबती उभरती ये यादें।
मैं भी चीरता इन परतों को...चुपचाप...
तुम्हे मिलने का प्रयत्न करता।
क्यों न करूँ मैं...साथ होने का प्रयास?
साथ है हम...इस एहसास को जी लेता|
कितनी परतें बिछ गईं समय की,
यादें दब गईं इन परतों के बोझ तले।।

Memories

So many layers of time lie in place,
Memories buried deep,
Beneath these layers of time.
However, at certain moments,
These memories rise to the surface,
Tearing apart the layers of time.
I too tear apart these layers—
Silently,
I attempt to meet you.
Why should I not try to be with you?
To experience the feeling of being with you
To live the feeling that we are together.
So many layers of time lie in place,
Memories buried deep,
Beneath these layers of time.

दूर हो तुम, पास भी हो तुम

दूर हो तुम...दूर हो तुम...
पास हो कर भी मेरे...दूर हो तुम|

कल्पना में भी दूर हो तुम...
पता नहीं कहाँ हो तुम।
मैं साहस करता कल्पना में भी...
समाप्त करने का इन दूरियों को।
लेकिन, जितने दूर हो तुम...
दिल में मेरे उतने ही पास हो तुम ।
जब मन चाहा छू लेता हूँ तुम्हें...
चुपचाप जी लेता हूँ तुम्हें।
व साहस करता...
समाप्त करने का इन दूरियों को।
तुम्हारी कल्पना भर...
भरती मेरे जीवन शून्य को,
परिवर्तित करती मेरे जीवन को।
व मैं जीवन के क्षणों को छू लेता...
करीब से जी लेता।।

You are far, yet so close

You are so far, you are so far,
You are so close, yet so far.
Even in my imagination, you are far.
I do not even know where you are
In my imagination,
I try to gather the courage to
bridge the distance between us.

You may be far,
But you are close to me in my heart.
I can touch you whenever I wish,
I can quietly live in your presence.
I summon the courage to bridge the distance between us.

The very thought of you eliminates the emptiness in my life,
Transforms my life.
And I can touch the moments of life,
And live in your presence closely.

कब से खोजता हूँ तुम्हें

कब से खोजता हूँ तुम्हे,
कहाँ कहाँ नहीं गया|
कितने स्वप्न देखे, इस खोज में,
स्वप्न में मिले भी तुम|
पर...साहस न जुटा पाया
साथ ले जाने का,
कह न पाया|
साथ चलो मेरे,
कह न पाया|
खोज रहा था तुम्हे,
परन्तु विश्वास है|
एक दिन,
असल जीवन में खोज पाऊँगा तुम्हे|
साहस जुटा पाऊँगा कुछ कहने का,
साथ ले जाने का तुम्हे||

How long have I been searching for you

How long have I been searching for you
How many places have I visited
How many times have I dreamt of you
I have even met you in my dreams.
But I could never gather the courage to take you with me.
I could never tell you,
'Come with me.'
I could never tell you,
'I have been looking for you.'
Yet I still believe
That one day,
I will find you in real life.
And I will gather the courage to ask you,
And take you with me.

■

I strongly believe that the role of counselling to support those facing mental health problems because of separation is very important, particularly in the first few years after the separation. We must have an organization and counsellors that can address this gap. A lot of people in Indian society have no idea about the problems of those estranged or divorced, their traumatic state of mind, and their emotional and psychological needs. Those who are divorced are perceived negatively and shunned by society. This needs to change, and a support system needs to be created for them.

Owing to our existing social mores, there is no support system for those undergoing the trauma of separation or estrangement. Forget our neighbours, even many of our relatives do not understand this. That is why I believe the concept of joint parenting is a good way to reduce the trauma faced by children of divorced couples. Given the impact that alienation from either parent can have on the child, making them choose between their father and mother without a considered evaluation of the possibilities of joint parenting may ultimately work against the child's best interests. However, the prevalent practice in the country is to grant custody to one parent, taking into account the welfare of the child.

In my view, children who have equal attachment and access to both parents experience better social and emotional development. Examples of shared parenting systems exist in a number of countries around the world, including the US, the UK, Australia, South Africa, and the Netherlands. With divorce rates on the rise in India these days, it's time our lawmakers gave serious thought to amending the Hindu Minority and Guardianship Act to alleviate the trauma that children of estranged parents undergo, owing to separation from one parent.

Any mother who creates seeds of doubt and negativity against a father in the minds of their children does not have the best interests of the children at heart. She couldn't have inflicted greater damage on her children! Any father who does that against a mother is equally guilty of this. Love is the greatest human need, and the children who don't get love from both their parents can end up lagging behind in the walk of life.

LIFE LESSONS

- Love is the greatest of human needs.
- Children who don't receive emotional support from both parents may, at times, find themselves falling behind in life.
- Joint parenting can be an effective way to lessen the trauma experienced by children of separated couples.
- Separated couples can remain friends.

9

Roadmap for the Future

This chapter outlines a clear vision for progress, charting practical steps and guiding principles to navigate challenges ahead. It serves as a blueprint for turning aspirations into achievable milestones, fostering growth, innovation, and long-term success.

Power of Giving Back to Society

One needs to look beyond the revenues and bottom lines of initiatives and focus instead on the social responsibility and goodwill one can garner through philanthropic efforts. The Tatas have a rich history of philanthropy and, over the years, have launched initiatives to benefit the community, such as building libraries, schools, and hospitals, and starting non-profit organizations. In fact, the Tata Memorial Hospital in Mumbai is one of the foremost and largest cancer treatment facilities in the country.

At Chemline, we are in the process of identifying the right area and thrust for our non-profit initiatives. We have decided that 50 per cent of our initiatives will be focused on charitable activities, and we are really serious and passionate about corporate social responsibility. We began by taking baby steps in the field of education. We launched scholarships for economically backwards, albeit meritorious, students. We have tied up with the Earth Saviours Foundation, which works in the area of upliftment of the poor. Their beneficiaries include those who were deserted by their parents or their loved ones. At their ashram, they take care of more than 1,000 such individuals who need shelter, food, and a healing touch.

Apart from giving back to the community, which comes under the purview of corporate social responsibility, the new buzzword in business responsibilities is the extent of support and commitment to environmental, social, and governance (ESG) obligations. This means that a company must not only be conscious of its impact on the environment but also be sensitive to the needs of society, while adhering to responsible norms of governance and environmentally friendly manufacturing practices. With standard parameters recognized around the world, ESG-related investments are measurable and therefore provide an objective assessment of a company's performance.

If your ESG score is high, it indicates that you are perceived as socially responsible and that corporations around the world would like to do business with you. Conversely, if you are not environmentally sustainable, companies, especially in the developed world, may not want to collaborate with you. At Chemline, we place particular emphasis on being environmentally friendly. Our lush, green campus is filled with shaded trees and foliage. We know that there is already a healthy precedent set by global business leaders, such as Microsoft co-founder Bill Gates, through the Bill and Melinda Gates Foundation, whose beneficiaries include communities in Indian states such as Uttar Pradesh and Bihar. Closer to home, Indian industrialist and IT pioneer Azim Premji has set benchmarks for others to emulate. In the financial year 2020–21, for instance, he donated ₹9,713 crore, equivalent to ₹27 crore a day, through the Azim Premji Foundation.[18] He routinely features in India's top philanthropist lists.

The philanthropy initiatives of the Ravindra Goel Charitable

---

[18]Punj, Vivek, 'Azim Premji Donated ₹27 Crore per Day. India's Top 10 Most Generous List Here', *Live Mint*, 28 October 2021, https://tinyurl.com/32cpdwum. Accessed on 13 August 2025.

Trust span diverse disciplines and audiences. They may focus on causes close to my heart, such as education for underprivileged children, or on areas such as environmental conservation and spirituality. One initiative could be about setting up a fellowship for meritorious science students engaged in path-breaking research. We might consider setting it up at my alma mater, IIT Delhi, where I completed my doctorate, or at Delhi University, which just celebrated its centenary in the presence of the Prime Minister.

We already support ISKCON through regular donations to fund their activities, including temple construction. We also offer scholarships, with a particular emphasis on supporting the education of girls. When we run a company or a factory, our aim should be to improve the environment rather than harm it. Our manufacturing facility in Dhaturi, near Murthal, is set within a lush, green campus. We have consciously designed our manufacturing processes to ensure that by-products cause minimal harm to the environment. For instance, we avoid processes that release solvents or emit harmful gases, opting instead for environmentally friendly alternatives. In our efforts to give back to the community, we have built toilets in schools located near our factory. We also focus on the needs of rural students in the surrounding areas, whether through paying their school fees or providing uniforms and textbooks.

Vision 2047

India will complete 100 years of independence in 2047. The government is working towards the goal of making India a developed country by then. At Chemline, we are in sync with this vision and are constantly innovating to help realize it. Times are changing at a frenetic pace; with evolving technology, people's requirements and lifestyles are transforming at a very fast clip. We have ended up producing and using products that we couldn't even imagine a few years back.

We will witness change at an even more rapid pace in the

years ahead. The products we manufactured earlier were created on the basis of demand, requirements, and the profit potential of that time. With changing times, the demand for these products has reduced, and some of them have become obsolete. At the same time, new innovations and exciting products have emerged to take their place. Judging by the way times have changed over the last

25 years, technology and consumer needs are likely to change even faster over the next 25. We may not even be able to imagine many of those changes today.

Over the years, I have realized that running an industry is a continuous journey of evolution. It is not enough to establish one plant or another; innovation must continue endlessly. To keep pace with the rapidly changing global environment, Chemline also needs to continuously adapt—either by introducing new products in our existing verticals or by exploring altogether new ones.

Today, I feel it has to be a never-ending journey to innovate and develop products that suit the needs of the times. For instance, we recently expanded into paper, as it is replacing plastic in many segments. Given India's dependence on imports for both basic paper and speciality paper, this was a strategic move. Similarly, we have expanded into eco-friendly products to replace single-use plastics and are developing materials that will enable the complete elimination of plastics in packaging. Sustainable food packaging is a buzzword these days, and Chemline has also contributed to propagating this thought. We have the innovation and wherewithal to produce sustainable, environmentally friendly products.

Today, in light of rapid changes in consumer tastes and industry requirements, I cannot predict how Chemline will look over the next 25 to 30 years. However, there is one thing that I am certain about—we will be doing many things that we are not doing today, and we will need to do many things differently to stay sustainable and profitable. We aim to be recognized as a great workplace with good HR practices. In the years ahead, our continuous pursuit of excellence will lead us to introduce new products and explore new markets. For us, evolution and innovation are not optional—they are the Chemline mantra in our vision for 2047.

Through our innovations, Chemline has provided an alternative to sustainable coating that was previously imported either from Germany or Japan. We are proud of our Indian origins and of the fact that Chemline is a home-grown success story. For more than three decades, since 1990, we have been making in India and are proudly wearing the 'Made in India' label.

As I envision the future for Chemline and look towards 2047, I can see that the future is bright and vibrant. We are just getting started! There are multiple milestones to be achieved, and my dream is that Chemline goes on to become a truly global multinational—one that is proudly made in India.

LIFE LESSONS

- At times, appointing a professional management team becomes imperative for family-run businesses.
- Entrepreneurs must give back to society.
- The new buzzword in business is investing in environmental, social, and governance (ESG) responsibilities.

With Mr P. Chidambaram, the then Union Minister of Commerce and Industry, visiting the Packaging Exhibition in Delhi in 1995

With Mr Sahib Singh Verma, former Chief Minister of Delhi, after he became a member of the 13th Lok Sabha in 1999

With Mrs Sheila Dikshit, the then Chief Minister of Delhi, at her residence in 2008 (third and fifth from left, respectively)

Receiving an award from Mr Manohar Lal Khattar, the then Chief Minister of Haryana, for outstanding performance in the field of exports at the State Level Export Award Ceremony held in Gurugram on 30 November 2016

Receiving the 'Company of the Year-2019 (Packaging)' award as the founder chairman and managing director of Chemline India Ltd from Mr Anurag Thakur, the then Union Minister of State for Finance and Corporate Affairs, at an event organized by Zee Business

Acknowledgements

My college friend Dilip Salwi, with whom I often shared stimulating intellectual discussions, was a prolific writer who would publish book after book. He once told me, 'Goel, you are a different person, you do not fully know yourself.' In the past, I had sponsored a compilation of quotations titled *Chemline Book of Quotable Science*.

Dilip began writing my biography in 2004, but sadly, he passed away soon after. Around the same time, I too nurtured the dream of making an intellectual contribution beyond my day-to-day business activities.

In 2019, I discussed this dream with another dear friend, Mr Ananda, author of *Tujhe Kya Chahiye Zindagi*. We had a few sittings for my biography, but unfortunately, he too passed away.

Later, in 2023, my friend Alexander introduced me to Dibakar Ghosh. Alexander played a pivotal role in setting this dream in motion. Throughout the writing of the book, he served as my first reader and sounding board, constantly reminding me not to let business responsibilities distract me from completing it.

My former associate and close friend, Ram Seshan, with whom I shared many in-depth discussions during our travels, offered invaluable feedback on the book's structure and patiently reviewed multiple drafts.

With Mr P. Chidambaram, the then Union Minister of Commerce and Industry, visiting the Packaging Exhibition in Delhi in 1995

With Mr Sahib Singh Verma, former Chief Minister of Delhi, after he became a member of the 13th Lok Sabha in 1999

With Mrs Sheila Dikshit, the then Chief Minister of Delhi, at her residence in 2008 (third and fifth from left, respectively)

Receiving an award from Mr Manohar Lal Khattar, the then Chief Minister of Haryana, for outstanding performance in the field of exports at the State Level Export Award Ceremony held in Gurugram on 30 November 2016